Supporting Inclusion

Other Books By the Author

Exceptional People: Lessons Learned from Special Education Survivors
Inclusion: Teachers' Perspectives and Practices

Supporting Inclusion

School Administrators' Perspectives and Practices

Faith Edmonds Andreasen

ROWMAN & LITTLEFIELD
Lanham • Boulder • New York • Toronto • Plymouth, UK

Published by Rowman & Littlefield
4501 Forbes Boulevard, Suite 200, Lanham, Maryland 20706
www.rowman.com

10 Thornbury Road, Plymouth PL6 7PP, United Kingdom

British Library Cataloguing in Publication Information Available

Library of Congress Cataloging-in-Publication Data

Andreasen, Faith E.
Supporting inclusion : school administrators' perspectives and practices / Faith Edmonds Andreasen.
pages cm.
ISBN 978-1-4758-0788-2 (cloth) — ISBN 978-1-4758-0789-9 (pbk.) —ISBN 978-1-4758-0790-5
(ebook)
1. Inclusive education—United States. 2. Students with disabilities—United States. 3. School administrators—United States. 4. School management and organization—United States. I. Title.
LC1201.A62 2014
371.9—dc23
2013049191

Contents

Acknowledgments

A book involving case studies can only be created through the cooperation of many people. On various occasions I reached out to friends, relatives and colleagues who then led me to a potential interviewee. Participants who voluntarily contributed to this endeavor frequently realized they had bitten off more than they originally intended as my interviews often required several hours of discussion followed by transcribing, editing, reviewing and more editing to bring these chapters to life.

I would therefore like to begin by thanking those anonymous participants who willingly gave of their limited time. With a strong commitment to their profession, the manner in which these individuals approach inclusion within their unique local community is inspiring and deserves thoughtful consideration and probable emulation. Next, I would like to thank those who led me to potential administrative participants—Susan Cardin-Hoffdahl, Mike Atkins, Jeff and Brenda Howard, Tom Gambino, Jeffrey Alejandro, Donna Rice, Kristen Guerricabetia and Judith Neill.

My husband, Russ, continues to be my most devoted supporter. When my one book grew into two, he unrelentingly gave his encouragement and support knowing my endeavor would require several more hours of research and writing. Similarly, Sheila Breen has been a trusted confidant and sounding board. Her ideas, guidance and input helped me get my thoughts on track on more than one occasion.

I remain grateful to Rowman & Littlefield, especially Tom Koerner, for reaching out to me and providing suggestions. I am also thankful to Caitlin Crawford for her correspondence, guidance and prompt responses.

Foreword

I vividly remember the day that I first met Dr. Faith Andreasen. An experienced principal, I had been hired to lead a large high school and was in need of a special education department chairperson. Disappointed with current applicants, I held interviews at an Arizona State job fair on the campus of ASU. Dr. Andreasen was the last person I interviewed that day.

Speaking with her, I quickly realized that she was not only well-versed in special education but she understood the needs, wants and desires of all students. She clearly possessed the requisite skills to lead a challenging department at a time when there were many changes taking place in education, especially in exceptional programs. With the pressures of No Child Left Behind, increased state and district standards coupled with the ever demanding challenges of preparing teachers to meet the needs of exceptional students, I could easily see that she had the passion and commitment to work with teachers, staff, parents—and especially the student—to bring out the best in students socially and academically.

As a principal I had just enough training to have an awareness of the inclusion model. However, I was not well-versed in how to build an inclusive program which was comprised of teams that could successfully implement sound instructional strategies while meeting the needs of all students. I quickly realized that Dr. Andreasen understood these strategies with all of their nuances. By providing the necessary teacher/student-centered professional development, she created an inclusive environment in which general and special educators as well as students and parents felt they were finally being given the tools needed to change the culture and maximize their potential.

As a direct result of Dr. Andreasen's efforts, student test scores improved tremendously. One can imagine the effect this had within her department, for individual teachers and parents— and especially for the students under her watch. In fact, her leadership as department chair helped the school come within a tenth of a point of being labeled an excelling school. I credit her for providing the necessary professional development that assisted teachers and students to perform at a level initially envisioned as only a dream. For me as the school principal, I was ecstatic—all the more so because this particular school had quite an extensive history of not meeting the district and state standards.

Supporting Inclusion: School Administrators' Perspectives and Practices depicts various aspects of inclusion from different administrators' viewpoints. Told by administrators who work in large and small districts across the country, this book describes their challenges and responsibilities as well as the do's and don'ts when building a successful inclusion program. Included are strategies to gain faculty buy-in, the need for meaningful teacher training, how to eke out time for collaboration, the best use of ancillary staff and instructional aides, and ways to provide technical support, to name a few. All of this is spelled out in an easy-to-understand format for administrators who want to learn of available options that will help them create a solid program. Each participant's main talking points are bulleted at the end of each chapter.

I would like to close with the following excerpt from Patrick M. Morley's book, *Walking with Christ in the Details of Life*, that best describes Dr. Andreasen:

> How pleasant to work side by side with a faithful person. They have a special quality about them. They don't moan and groan about how hard life is, though it is equally hard for them as for any of the rest of us. No, instead they are dependably reliable. You know them. They are the ones you never doubt will get the job done. You don't know how they do it, but consider it done.

You see, Faith builds positive relationships that yield a high degree of productivity. She understands what it takes to give of herself so that others will become successful. I have learned a lot from her and so will all the readers of this book. Dr. Andreasen's experience and insight to special education and the inclusion model is exceptional. I highly recommend this book for all school administrators and aspiring administrators as well. I believe you will find this book to be a valuable resource as you delve into the special education arena.

To Faith, I find myself very fortunate to have worked for you!
I wish you continued success.

Tom Hernandez
Administrator for Human Resources
Glendale Union High School District, Glendale, Arizona

Preface

As I was interviewing teachers for the complement to this book, *Inclusion: Teachers' Perspectives and Practices,* they made it very clear that everything that does or does not happen on their school campus is a result of their administrator's priorities. If keeping athletic teams in high standing is important, new equipment is bought. If updating technology is essential, new hardware or software is ordered and installed. If childhood obesity is a concern, machines with sugary snacks are replaced with ones that provide water, juice and healthy snacks. Similarly, if inclusion is a priority, research-based strategies such as training and mentoring are provided in order to make a seamless transition from a segregated to a more integrated campus.

My own experience transitioning an inner-city high school environment from a pullout resource to an inclusive one was frequently harangued in my doctorate coursework. The school's inclusion cadre was created by a group of concerned educators who were dismayed at the disproportionate pullout resource schedules imposed upon the exceptional student population by an administration that continually refused to comply with state and federal laws. The school's top administrators persistently cited the financial cost to the school as the reason for their blanket policy of resource classes for all students with a disability.

However, special educators consistently discussed the ultimate cost of ignoring individual students' school programs and subsequent post-secondary life, believing that the price was incalculable. The blanket policy clearly did not respect the students' rights, individual education plan (IEP), or least-restrictive environment (LRE) laws. Thus, four core special education team members reached out to their general education colleagues with the intention of educating them on what disabled meant and the students' academic capabilities. The intention was to gain buy-in to the inclusion concept.

The special educators who spearheaded the inclusion project began by identifying the problem—the need for an inclusion program to legally coincide with students' IEPs and to honor their LRE. Next, potential general educators who were already willingly and enthusiastically including exceptional students were identified. Then team members brainstormed how general educators would be trained, which model the inclusion program would mimic, short- and long-term goals and the support needed from administrators. During the first formal inclusion meeting, the targeted general education faculty members had an open forum to ask questions enabling them to better understand the special education population. At the meeting's conclusion, they agreed the concept of inclusion sounded proactive and doable, and the cadre agreed to meet at regular intervals.

It was decided that additional training would be provided via off- and onsite professionals in support of the inclusion mission. It was also agreed that each team (for example the math team and science team) was free to implement what they learned through the cadre training according to their own personalities and styles. Thus, the co-teaching content teams would agree amongst themselves how they would implement their daily lesson plans, minimizing discord. While some minor adjustments needed to be made as the school year progressed, this approach ensured each person had a voice regarding how they envisioned their part as the inclusion program progressed.

To encourage reluctant administrators to agree to initiate this inclusion process, fifty freshmen special education students that the team felt would succeed in the general education environment were identified. The criteria used to determine who these students were included grades, attendance and attitude. Already scheduled into electives of their choice, the four content areas into which they were to be included were social studies, English, science and mathematics. The intent was to start small and gradually increase student numbers in subsequent years by 5 percent, making the transition to inclusion feasible. Once the short-term vision was determined, the one-, two-, and three-year benchmarks were delineated. Specifically, the requirements for additional faculty to accommodate a growing inclusion program were discussed, plans for the continued identification of future inclusion students were examined and how to implement support for the initial group of students in subsequent years were considered.

The proposal to administrators was simple. The general education classes implementing inclusion would have ten special education and twenty general education students per period. The special education students would be placed on the inclusion teachers' schedule first, and then the general education students would be scheduled around them. In order to facilitate planning and accommodations, it was recommended that the co-teaching teams have a common planning period. Additionally, to accommodate students who were not selected for the initial inclusion pilot program, the special education teacher would teach one resource class as needed.

When the inclusion proposal was presented to administrators, the main points addressed were those known to be important issues, those that make a real difference in the day-to-day operation of the school and that have a statistically significant positive cumulative outcome. When compared to their segregated resource peers, it was projected there would be improved criterion reference test (CRT) scores, reduced behavior referrals, increased attendance, fewer failures and eventually an increased graduation rate. The proposal was agreed to, and the next year's data revealed exciting results as significant gains by the students in the inclusion environment were evidenced. CRT scores rose approximately 30 percent, behavior referrals dropped by nearly 80 percent, and attendance increased by approximately 20 percent, far exceeding the established goals!

The positive data resulted in the encouraged administrators making inclusion a priority, supporting its evolution and permitting more students to be included each year. An example of support occurred when a stipend for the cadre was approved so team members could meet bi-monthly after school for planning time during which members collaboratively used data to drive decision making on behalf of each student. The cadre also brainstormed solutions to issues that occurred in the classroom, drawing on their colleagues' expertise and implementing agreed upon solutions into their daily activities. The collective goal of increasing student performance by providing an environment that would afford multiple learning opportunities thereby enhancing student skills was being met.

As this story portrays, strong, gifted, dogged administrators are needed. Teachers desire administrative support and students desire the opportunity to be part of the school instead of "those kids" or "the special education students." Providing moments for all students to participate in interesting, meaningful, dynamic classes should be a standard practice. Sharing the responsibility for inclusion through purposeful preparation, resolute commitment and firm accountability enables all parties to improve their performance and maximize their potential. By contributing to a cause bigger than themselves, administrators have the ability to develop a resourceful staff whose daily actions are efficacious, gratifying and fortified as a result of their synergy.

Introduction

Remember your first administrative job when you thought, "I have arrived!" You'd arrived all right—to the pinnacle of constant pressure and immense responsibility. You were enthusiastic, idealistic and believed ALL things were possible. You believed you could give hope to those you served. When you initially felt inspired to become a leader, you exerted a great amount of effort to obtain administration certification. Your goal was to have a broader reach to help your colleagues improve their skills so they could have a greater impact on the lives of their students.

Once certification was attained, you found you must comply with the dictates of politicians, appease the orations of parents, meld the ideals of your school with the district's vision and be readily available for every staff member who must talk to you "now." You knew this was part of leadership and had experienced it in your practicum, but you hadn't experienced the full intensity of being under a microscope daily. You found the experience to be draining on both your professional and personal life. Yet it was oddly invigorating as well.

After all, what is more worthwhile than investing time and energy into others with the intention of everyone achieving their maximum potential, of positively impacting the lives of both teachers and students? This is clearly a win-win situation for everyone. Gifted administrators innately understand the correlation between their relationship with staff members and the fulfillment of their collective outcomes. By devoting time to listening and by providing support via materials, collaboration and mentorship, administrators significantly influence their staff's willingness to go the extra mile.

It's not that every idea brought to the table by an administrator is embraced, quite the contrary. Teachers often voice their dissent and concerns over practically every policy change. Yet, and perhaps because of, an administrator's willingness to hear honest opinions, a collective resolution to the policy is derived and teachers feel they have ownership of that policy.

PURPOSE

Administrators operate within a complex fluctuating system in which they are required to demand optimal performance from their staff as dictated by the Common Core State Standards (CCSS). Required to make several dozen decisions daily, sometimes lacking complete and accurate information, administrators are expected to effectively address issues with a certainty that their decisions will result in positive outcomes. In brief, teachers expect their administrators to effectively lead, which is measured in part via perceptions of how often their leaders are available and responsive to their needs. Likewise, administrators desire to be effective leaders; however, they often face obstacles from external sources that are sometimes out of their control.

For instance, Administrator 1 works in a district comprised of many older school buildings that lack adequate space for computer labs or that are not structurally able to accommodate the wiring needed for new technology. This clearly impacts teachers' abilities to prepare their students for work in a global community. Likewise, it impacts the teachers' and administrators' ability to have up-to-date information immediately at their disposal subsequently affecting their decision-making abilities. Another issue out of an administrator's control is the need to hire staff members but not finding an applicant with a specific skill set. For instance, paraprofessionals demonstrate certain competencies when they pass the ParaPro Assessment required by the No Child Left Behind Act or possess an associate's degree. Nonetheless, they must sometimes be paired with a student whose disability is outside the realm of their knowledge.

Fortunately, administrators also have unique opportunities to develop vital programs by working with issues that are within their control. Inclusion is one such program, but the conundrum is how this should be accomplished. A great deal of thought and collaboration is required to train a team of teachers to effectively implement the inclusion model. This is especially true when today's teachers already feel overwhelmed by current requirements to develop a curriculum and scramble to find resources to meet the new CCSS.

This book was therefore written for the purpose of delineating the strategies various administrators are implementing to make inclusion a successful reality. How they overcome obstacles such as budgetary constraints and the resultant loss of paraprofessionals, squeeze out time for general and special educators to have collaboration time and other logistical issues are discussed. Additionally, how inclusive issues such as ascertaining whether full- or partial-inclusion is appropriate, where aides should be placed to maximize their effectiveness and how time is eked out for training is described.

AUDIENCE

Supporting Inclusion: School Administrators' Perceptions and Practices is written primarily for university faculty and practitioners in the field of education and the social sciences, including current teachers, ancillary staff, administrators and policymakers. This book, well-suited as a supplementary text for undergraduate, graduate and continuing education classes, captures the multifaceted challenges faced by administrators as inclusion is implemented across our nation's schools. It delineates what administrators from elementary to high school levels say works, challenges they face and the specific support and resources they attempt to provide. Conversely, it clarifies what administrators view as barriers, detracting from the school-wide vision.

PARTICIPANTS

Administrators from the elementary to the high school levels, district office and Department of Education contributed to this book. The table here provides an easy reference regarding each administrator's experience, school rank and student population. The school rank is rounded to the nearest 5 percent with 1 percent being the top and 99 percent being the bottom. Not applicable (n/a) is placed in the column "# of years in current school" for Administrators 1, 3 and 7 because they were working at the Department of Education and at the district level at the time they were interviewed.

Similarly, not applicable (n/a) is printed in the "number of years in the current district" for Administrator 7, who has recently led two cyber schools. "Student population in the current school" has two numbers for Administrator 3, noting the two high schools he led. Likewise, the two numbers for Administrator 7 refers to his two cyber schools. Under "% ESE," 10 percent of the student population in both of Administrator 3's schools was exceptional. In contrast, Administrator 7's two cyber schools were more diverse with about 8 percent of the population in his first school and 16 percent of the student population in his second school requiring special education support.

Please note that "level" indicates the level in which the administrator refers to during the interview. For example, Administrator 3 currently works at the district level but details how he led his two high schools when he served as a principal. Administrators 4 and 5 work in a small school; thus, they simultaneously serve at the district and the school level. Administrator 7 refers to his brick-and-mortar experience as well as his cyber school experience; however, the table delineates his cyber school experience.

It is important to acknowledge that administrators work with diverse populations in a multitude of settings. Thus, the school ranking noted in the table below does not necessarily reflect the participants' knowledge, skills and abilities. For instance, some administrators have large populations of newly immigrated refugee students who score low on the state standardized test incorrectly implying that teachers are unskilled and the leadership is lacking. Other administrators lead teachers who instruct large populations of "privileged" students in affluent communities.

Table of Administrator Interviewee Information

Admin Name	Level	School Or Dist. Rank	Region	# of Yrs in Ed.	# of Yrs Teach-ing	# of Yrs in Current District	# of Yrs in Current School	Student Pop. in Current Dist. Or School	% ESE
1	DOE	50%	Pacific	36	9	36	n/a	13,860	6
2	HS	10%	Pacific	17	14	3	1	3700	11
3	HS	15& 25%	So. West	41	19	26	n/a	1200/ 2000	10
4	Dis & HS	30%	Rock Mt	23	6	17	17	107	13
5	Dis & EL	15%	Rock Mt	24	3	9	9	117	16
6	MS	75%	So. East	14	4.5	5	4	650	11
7	C-HS	n/a	No. East	18	7.5	n/a	2	500/129	8/16
8	Dis	25%	Midwest	38	n/a	30	n/a	1800	11

Notes: Under Level, DOE = Department of Education; HS = high school; C-HS – cyber high school; MS=middle school; DIS = district office; EL=Elementary.
Under School or District Rank, the two percentages for Administrator 3 refers to the two high schools he led. Administrators 4 and 5 work for the same "small school" district and participated in a joint interview; their percentages refer to their schools. The two percentages for Administrator 7 refers to the two cyber-schools he led.
Student population, Administrator 1 = the number of students in her district; Administrator 3 = the number of students in the two high schools respectively; Administrator 7 = the number of students in his two cyber-schools; Administrator 8 = the student population in her district.
% ESE, Administrator 4 = percent in his high school; Administrator 5 = percent in her elementary school; Administrator 8 = percent in his two cyber-schools respectively.

High test scores might therefore inaccurately infer that these administrators are more capable than their colleagues who work in lower ranking schools.

The table therefore only depicts the environment within which the participants work and is not meant to imply one administrator is more skilled than
the other. Also, great care has been taken to protect the identity of the participants. Similarities between the interviewee and someone you know are pure-
ly coincidental.

ORGANIZATION

Supporting Inclusion: School Administrators' Perceptions and Practices is a
comprehensive compilation of case studies obtained from administrators
from U.S. territories and states. The U.S. map regions define the boundaries
for each area. Please note that Hawaii, Alaska, and the territory of Guam are
in the Pacific region. Each chapter herein, which can be read in any order,
describes one administrator's perspective and the context within which inclusion practices are executed.

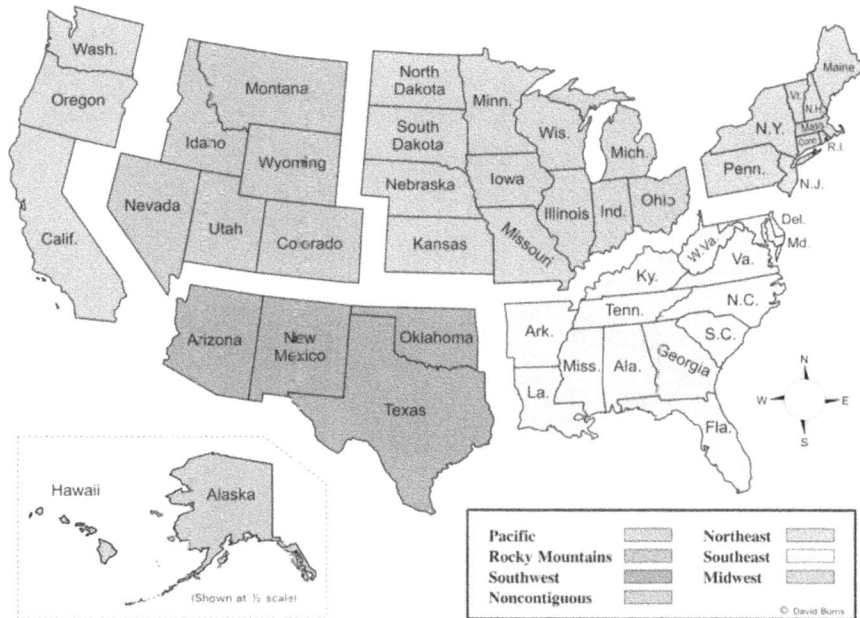

U.S. Map Regions

Each administrator's contextual framework is followed by detailed information regarding pertinent issues such as the challenges one faces when
transitioning the school's structure to support the inclusive philosophy, how
instructional aides' talents are maximized and how data is used to drive
decision-making. Please note the terms special education student, special
needs student, student with a disability, student with an exceptionality, stu-

dent with an IEP, and exceptional student are used interchangeably. Also, some administrators refer to their classified staff members as instructional aides (IAs) while others refer to them as paraprofessionals. Each chapter closes with a summary of the administrator's talking points.

Finally, administrators recognize that their teachers are the backbone of the school. As one administrator stated, "The demands that are placed on them exceed anything seen before in our country." Understanding and meeting teachers' needs so they can perform their duties responsibly is of utmost importance. Thus, there is a complementary book to this titled *Inclusion: Teachers' Perspectives and Practices* that detail the challenges that teachers face, strategies implemented to overcome these challenges, what they say works and what they need. I invite you to read both books to gain a well-rounded understanding of the responsibilities and challenges faced by each group (teachers and administrators) and how they are successfully overcome.

Chapter One

Administrator 1: Pacific Region

Administrator 1 has been an educator in the Pacific region for approximately thirty-six years. She began her career working for four years as a speech language therapist. She then became a teacher for the deaf and hard of hearing for nine years. Finally, she worked at the Department of Education (DOE) Division of Special Education until her recent retirement. While at the DOE she oversaw various programs including those for the deaf and hard of hearing, itinerant, speech and language and early intervention working with special needs children from birth to three years of age. She completed the last five years of her career in the special education compliance department.

Approximately 6 percent of the students in Administrator 1's district receive special services. This is well below the national average and implies students are not over-identified. Misidentification is avoided by administering a language assessment to the various ethnic groups who live in the district. Mechanisms are in place, such as home language surveys, that identify students as English as a second language (ESL) learner when applicable.

Students who are identified as ESL receive immersion courses for at least two years so they can become conversant in English. This district has an exceptional record of identifying and not confusing ESL students with the special education population. "It cannot be said that misidentification never occurs, but those instances are minimal."

RESOURCES

Speaking from her many years of experience with the deaf and hard of hearing, Administrator 1 believes inclusion is beneficial. She expounds that educators need to be given the correct supports such as interpreters, assistive technology boards or training. Doing so is a positive tactic that benefits all students. While she avers that inclusion may not be appropriate for every child, she does believe it is important for all students to be educated in the regular education environment to the greatest extent possible. "It helps them to feel normal and accepted."

BENEFITS OF INCLUSION

Administrator 1 stresses that children with learning disabilities should have their issues addressed in an environment that is conducive to positive outcomes. This is especially true when it comes to social development. Developing social skills occurs in a more meaningful manner when special education students have modeling from their general education peers versus when they are segregated. Her district's leaders believe that the least restrictive environment (LRE) for most of their students with disabilities is the general education classroom and that their individual education plans (IEPs) reflect this. Inclusion is supported through collaboration among general education teachers, special education teachers, service providers and parents.

INCLUDING STUDENTS WITH EMOTIONAL BEHAVIOR DISORDERS

Administrator 1's district's programs have been very successful in terms of placing students with emotional behavior disorders (EBD) into general education classrooms. They are placed with their general education peers when they are able to demonstrate appropriate social skills per their IEP. "The success of the EBD population hinges on having the proper supports in place."

When EBD students are segregated, they are placed in a self-contained classroom with a certified, highly qualified teacher who understands their needs. These needs are addressed in an environment that the student views as a safe haven. Once they demonstrate the ability to comply with the rules in a segregated safe environment, they are gradually transitioned, when appropriate and in accordance with their IEP, to the regular education class. Administrator 1 stresses that the goal is always to place students with disabilities in the regular education environment to the greatest extent possible.

CHALLENGES IMPLEMENTING THE INCLUSIVE MODEL

Administrator 1 states there are multiple obstacles for administrating and implementing an ideal inclusive environment. For example, some secondary schools in her district have block scheduling, which prevents time for staff collaboration during the school day. Budgetary constraints reduce the ability for teachers to receive compensation to meet before or after school. Also, the inability to employ sufficient ancillary staff prevents therapy services from being consistently delivered, which in turn thwarts timely student progress.

Administrator 1's district has not been affected by the economy in the same manner as most. Hence, paraprofessionals have not been laid off in great numbers; "If they leave, it is for personal reasons." This district has general as well as special education paraprofessionals who work in one of two categories. Their assignments occur at the discretion of the school administrator.

One category of paraprofessionals works on a full-time basis while the other category is part-time. Most of the one-on-one part-time paraprofessionals are funded through a grant. In the pullout resource classes, there can be a paraprofessional for the whole classroom as well as a one-on-one paraprofessional who is assigned to a particular student. As one would assume, one-on-one paraprofessionals follow their assigned student from class to class.

INCLUSIVE PROGRAMMING

Administrator 1 states that usually there is not a dedicated counselor for the special education population; counselors usually work with all students. However, there are a few schools who have decided to have one counselor responsible for the special education students' schedules. Thus, counselor assignments vary depending on the individual school.

Administrator 1 notes co-teaching does not exist in its truest form. However, attempts have been made between teachers to implement the co-teaching model. This occurs with approval from their local administrator. Co-teaching is defined as two teachers collaborating and working together with clusters of students. They share in the design, organization, delivery and assessment of instruction within a common physical space. The goal is to increase student learning. The key to a successful co-teaching model is that both teachers are actively engaged in all facets of instruction (Eastern Washington Co-Teaching Consortium, n.d.).

Administrator 1 believes both the co-teaching and the partial inclusion models have their benefits. Sometimes, co-teaching works due to the proximity of the teachers, and sometimes because one teacher has more resources than another teacher. In her district, co-teaching occurs based on teacher initiative.

Co-teaching is considered to be beneficial for special education students "because they work harder to prove themselves and are privy to an appropriate social environment." When included students have an obvious disability such as a hearing or orthopedic impairment, the general education students benefit because they learn acceptance and tolerance. When Administrator 1 was a teacher, she implemented both the parallel and team teaching models. In the parallel teaching model, both teachers instruct the same information, but they divide the class into two groups and conduct the lessons simultaneously. In the team teaching model, both teachers deliver instruction simultaneously, and instruction becomes more than turn taking.

Because inclusive strategies are teacher initiated, Administrator 1 has not seen any data regarding the impact inclusion has had on academic or social outcomes; as of this date, neither teachers nor administrators have gathered this information. Thus, there have been no comparisons of pre- or post-inclusive implemented strategies. However, teachers have commented that they were surprised how well special education students behave in the general education environment as compared to their behavior when segregated from their peers.

As the program coordinator for the deaf and hard of hearing, Administrator 1 was responsible for overseeing interpreters and teachers at three school sites. Each site was staffed with one to three teachers who worked with paraprofessionals or interpreters. To ensure a cohesive vision was adopted at each site, she made weekly visits to assist and collaborate with individuals and groups as needed. She would also hold meetings with the site administrator to address their concerns or issues.

Additionally, Administrator 1 held monthly meetings regarding programmatic operational issues that pertained specifically to her department. This strategy helped everyone focus on the same goal. Administrator 1 noted that fulfilling her administrative responsibilities within this structure minimized problems. Because of the mechanism she put in place to address issues as they arose, she was able to anticipate and discuss issues in a timely manner. To enhance timely resolution, she would meet with her teachers, her paraprofessionals and her interpreters separately. This enabled her to listen, discuss and address their issues separately, concurrently allowing her to stay on top of issues as they arose and resolve them appropriately.

Regarding compliance, Administrator 1 affirms that school personnel were very cognizant of their responsibilities and germanely fulfilled them. They were eager to comply with the Individuals with Disabilities Education Act (IDEA) and other special education laws. Her compliance officers did not approach site educators regarding deficient concerns in an adversarial manner. Their goal was to collaborate and resolve issues as they emerged from the compliance reviews. She found school personnel to be very accommodating and cooperative.

The timeframe for compliance reviews was one week and involved various activities. Some of these activities included a comprehensive examination of cumulative files, interviews and observations in the classroom, on the playground and in the cafeteria. Undergoing the review process for the first time was a learning process for first year teachers. In spite of feeling some apprehension, gaps that needed to be addressed were mostly met with an open mind.

If an IEP stated a certain service was to be provided within the classroom, Administrator 1 and her officers would visit the classroom to see if that service was indeed being provided as delineated. Parent interviews were also part of the compliance process; one full day was devoted to meeting with them. Regretfully, surveying general education teachers regarding how supported they felt by special education faculty or personnel was not part of the process. At the conclusion of the week's review, administrators were debriefed. Sometimes teachers were involved; however, usually the administrator met with her teachers after being fully debriefed by the compliance officers.

SPECIAL EDUCATION TERMINOLOGY, SERVICES AND STRATEGIES

Teachers are aware of basic acronyms that special educators use such as free and appropriate education (FAPE), individualized education plan and least restrictive environment. In the elementary environment the IEP coordinator (at the secondary level it is the consulting resource teacher [CRT]) ensures the appropriate general education teacher(s) have a copy of the IEP and an explanation regarding the nuances of the child's disability. Thus, accommodations are discussed and programming needs are in place prior to that child entering the classroom. If there are any questions or concerns, experienced general education teachers know who to go to for information. Moreover, special education personnel reach out to all teachers to ensure they know the process.

Training regarding special education issues is continually provided by the Division of Special Education. For example, a school might have a specific population, such as students on the autism spectrum disorder scale. The principal sends a memorandum to the assistant superintendent of special education requesting training in autism strategies for his faculty and paraprofessionals. Technical assistant (TAs) specialists are sent to address this need.

If a student requires any ancillary service such as occupational or physical therapy, the appropriate therapist provides direct therapy, or consults and collaborates with the general education teacher. The therapist ensures that the teacher understands how that student's disability affects his or her ability to perform in the classroom. It is expected that the appropriate special education person will collaborate with the general education teacher so the general educator clearly understands how to comply with the student's IEP goals and objectives. Administrator 1 notes that in her district speech and language services are not adequately staffed. The lack of a competitive salary coupled with a large caseload makes recruiting difficult.

STANDARDIZED TESTS

Administrator 1's district does not view or use the state standardized test as a high stakes exam. She believes standardized testing does not convey any useful information to service the special education child. However, she believes that special education students should participate in any testing that their general education counterparts do as a matter of their "right to access."

ATTAINING BUY-IN TO THE INCLUSION MODEL

Administrator 1 has seen a positive shift in the general educators' attitude and acceptance of inclusion. This shift has occurred because they have had time to digest the need as well as the implications. "They have gone through the growing pains that a shift in culture requires and have reached the point that they understand inclusive practice is the law. They no longer ask, 'Why should I?' or 'Why do I have to?'"

A large part of the teachers' buy-in has been due to the support, training and awareness that the Department of Education has provided. Training sometimes occurs before the school year begins and other times it occurs as the need arises. If the school administrator or faculty feel there is a critical need for specific training, it can be requested at that time. Some groups, such as those who work with autistic students, receive training on an ongoing basis. Other teachers receive training as a refresher.

General education teachers comment that they must dedicate more time and thought to creating lesson plans when working with inclusive populations. They generally do not complain about this task. Administrator 1 has heard comments that, when an activity was implemented to accommodate a special education student, that strategy ultimately benefited other members of the class. "General education students often enthusiastically participate and ask if they can do more activities like the one they just enjoyed."

Administrator 1 emphatically emphasizes a crucial piece of success in any program is leadership by each school's principal. "Leadership and training are key to affecting employees' opinions." Knowing which principals are not on board provides the Department of Education personnel a target audience for mandatory training.

PARENT SATISFACTION AND TECHNOLOGY

Per the state Parent Satisfaction Survey, parents of students with disabilities in Administrator 1's district rate their level of satisfaction with the programs and services their children receive at the 50th percentile. Teacher communication with parents occurs through customary channels. These include progress reports, communication books, parent conferences, individual meetings with teachers and occasionally Internet correspondence.

Every school has access to the Internet; however, the number of computers available for use in the classroom varies from school to school. Administrators are provided with laptops for their use. Yet, not every teacher and not every classroom has a computer. Furthermore, every school does not have a computer lab. Often, students can only gain access to computers on a rotating basis.

Some of the district's technological challenges come in the form of budgetary constraints and older buildings. The budget affects the district's ability to acquire expensive equipment. Older schools lack adequate space for computer labs; some buildings are not structurally able to accommodate the wiring needed for technology. The district's information technology personnel continue to work on upgrading school buildings so that they are all capable of supporting technological advances.

PEER TUTORS

Peer tutors are utilized in the inclusive environment, but using the buddy system varies from teacher to teacher. Peer tutoring is viewed as a beneficial strategy for both the tutor and the tutee. The tutor is provided with the opportunity to share knowledge and learn leadership skills. For special education students, it provides the opportunity for building confidence and success and learning appropriate social skills. "Matching students appropriately is a critical part to the success of the peer tutor model."

TEACHER EVALUATIONS

Teacher evaluations have been recently updated in Administrator 1's district. The evaluation does take into account teaching students with diverse needs such as accommodating for special education students and students who are culturally and linguistically diverse. The district is committed to understanding these challenges and supporting their personnel via continuous and consistent collaboration and training.

CREATING A SUPPORTIVE CLASSROOM ENVIRONMENT

The classroom environment is altered to accommodate special education students as needed. For example, students with ADHD are strategically seated among their peers in a place that limits distractions and is most conducive to everyone's learning. Furthermore, students in wheelchairs or who need orientation and mobility considerations are accommodated for an on-going basis.

As was previously mentioned, teacher attitudes toward inclusion have shifted and become more positive because of the training the district provides. Thus, differentiated instruction is used in the classrooms. Most of the elementary schools have recently implemented positive behavioral interventions and supports. There is ongoing collaboration between general education teachers, special education teachers, service providers and parents to ensure that supports and accommodations are provided.

STRESS

The stress level felt as the district works to comply with NCLB mandates ranges from minimal to moderate. To support administrators, the district holds a leadership academy during the summer, usually before school opens. The academy provides an opportunity for principals to learn new teaching and management skills and to share solutions or ideas to challenges they have faced as an administrator. Principals also receive training on a variety of special education topics. "While expectations due to NCLB are higher, training helps mitigate the stress."

INCLUSION'S IMPACT

Administrator 1 believes the way schools practice inclusion has a positive impact on all students and for all teachers. Special education students rise to the occasion while general education students become more accepting and tolerant of others with differences. Special education teachers as well as their general education counterparts benefit when they can collaborate and orchestrate a well-developed lesson. Administrator 1 concludes by emphasizing that, "The success of an inclusive program, and any program for that matter, begins at the top. Everything starts with a leader's vision and direction. Only then can everything else fall in line. This is very critical."

Note: Administrator 1's Talking Points are listed with Administrator 2 as both are in the Pacific Region.

Chapter Two

Administrator 2: Pacific Region

Administrator 2 works at a high school in the Pacific region that ranks in the top 10 percent of her state. There are approximately 3,700 students on her campus and of those about 11 percent are special education students. Administrator 2 states education is a second career for her. She has been a teacher at the elementary, middle school and high school levels. She taught for fourteen years in general education and worked with students who were included. She taught in the elementary school for five years, English and science at the middle school level for seven years, and then moved into the secondary environment.

Administrator 2 began working as an administrator in 2009. She began at the district level, working special assignment supporting four high schools' special education departments as an instructional coach partnering with the program specialist. During that time, Administrator 2 handled instruction and the program specialist dealt with compliance. In this assignment, she worked with special education teachers regarding co-teaching strategies to help them become more effective implementing this model.

Administrator 2 states that, as an instructional specialist, she saw many credentialed, professional master degreed teachers stand in the back of the classroom copying homework and notes off the board for students. "I knew this was a waste of their talent and skill." To help teachers better understand how to effectively provide access to the curriculum for students with disabilities, she brought Richard Villa, a renowned co-teaching trainer who has authored several books, to her district to train her faculty. They learned how to implement research-based strategies in their classrooms, which began the trend of implementing co-teaching on her campuses.

Administrator 2's colleagues implied that she was going to remain in her position at the district and continue developing with the co-teaching program. However, she was reassigned and placed at her current high school where she has been delighted to see some of the fruits of her district-level efforts. Her "lofty mission" is for special educators to become "masters of access" and general educators to become "masters of content." She believes if these two "masters" work well together, then there is a better chance of all students having access to the same curriculum.

IDENTIFYING STUDENTS AS SPECIAL NEEDS

Administrator 2 thinks the majority of the students who are identified as needing special education services are correctly placed. However, she believes some students are on an individual education plan (IEP) who do not need services. "Students and parents are resistant to being exited from the special education program because they like having the safety net that an IEP provides." Administrator 2 does see fewer accommodations occurring for these students and ensures they are placed in the least restrictive environment; nonetheless, they remain on the census as IEP students. She regrets that exiting students from special education services is currently not a primary goal of parents or teachers.

Administrator 2 opines that she still hears general educators comment that students with special needs do not belong in regular education classrooms. "Their perception is that special education students interrupt the flow of the regular class and that they take away from general education students who have a right to education." They fear that their general education students are not getting what is needed because of a small subset of students on IEPs being present.

Administrator 2 admits her early understanding of placing students with exceptionalities in various educational environments were not well-formed. She had the mentality that if a student was disruptive to her setting, the annoyance could be eliminated by sending the student back to the special education teacher with the thought, "You take him." This held true until she personally experienced her son needing an IEP. His fourth grade teacher called her and said, "I cannot handle your son and need him out of my class because he has too many behavior problems."

Administrator 2 swapped students with this teacher and therefore taught her own child. Intuitively, she knew what he needed to be successful "because I was his mom." The realization came to her that if her own son needed certain supports, then how many other students needed them? "I recognized everyone would be more successful if I made simple instructional adjustments for all students that I was making for my son. It absolutely changed my way of thinking as far as what my expectations were."

Going through the process of having her son identified as a student with a disability and learning how to address his unique needs "absolutely changed my perspective regarding how I wanted to treat other students." Her viewpoint today has shifted greatly from the day she first entered the classroom. She embraces the opportunity to work with all students and accepts them with open arms. "There is no reason I cannot create an activity to help all students understand a concept even if the activity was not originally in the lesson plan."

Administrator 2 believes when she became more competent as an instructor, she then became more open to the inclusion concept. "I understood that success is not defined by all students doing all things the same way." So, her "embarrassing" initial perception evolved.

OBSTACLES TO INCLUSION

Administrator 2 describes budgetary constraints, the lack of resources, the loss of aides due to the bad economic times, parent misperceptions regarding the power a school administrator has and teachers' misperceptions of the legal ramifications if an IEP is not followed as obstacles to creating an inclusive school. "The budget is a big issue. Contrary to the public's perception, the special education budget is not loaded with a bottomless pot of money." Surprisingly, special educators often do not have the same resources as general education teachers. "I am appalled; special education is not the deep pocket people think it is." She believes litigation lends to this misperception.

"Special education students often do not have access to the same curriculum." Administrator 2 is distraught that the accepted mentality is that the huge textbook for a course is given to all teachers and they are supposed to "make it work." She believes this is backwards. A solution is for educators to look at the standards that are most critical and determine the materials needed to address those standards. If information from the textbook can be utilized then that is great; otherwise additional resources should be incorporated. "Access to curricular resources is a huge need that should not go unaddressed."

Regarding the budget and cutting instructional assistants (IAs), "that loss is definitely felt." There is not enough instructional support for students who would benefit but Administrator 2 feels like her hands are tied. "Many times we know in our heart that what is best for a student is not what can be offered per the free and appropriate public education (FAPE) law." FAPE does not delineate what is best or guarantee that the student is going to reach his maximum potential; it only says progress towards the goals will be made in the least restrictive environment. Thus, many things are not provided from which students could benefit.

Parents mistakenly believe school administrators have the power to make decisions that serve the best interest of their child 100 percent of the time. This is not true because the district does not always have the power to back up prudent decisions. For example, Administrator 2 has been told to not make any decisions under FAPE that will cost the district money without getting district approval ahead of time. She is to table the decision; thus, as an administrator she has no freedom to make grounded decisions with the assurance that they will be implemented.

Moreover, Administrator 2 cannot say that the IEP meeting is being postponed because that will look like the decision is coming from the district and not from the IEP team. This discouraging position leaves her with the option of saying she is tabling the meeting or saying "no" to IEP team decisions. She feels caught between a rock and a hard place, "and this is all because of the budget. If the money with there, I would have a freer hand."

The perception of teachers is another obstacle. Administrator 2 states she has actually heard teachers say, "I don't care if there is an IEP, I am not following it." She has also seen administrators pull students from a class and place them with a teacher who would follow the IEP instead of holding the noncompliant teacher accountable. "The administrator did this because it was easier than dealing with the hassle of teacher accountability—writing up the teacher, exerting the effort to follow through, and dealing with the parents. This is viewed as an easy fix."

Another issue on Administrator 2's campus is the unwillingness of general educators to work with BRIDGE (functional level) students who attend electives such as art, music, or dance for one period per day. If an issue arises, that student is sent back to the BRIDGE teacher. "That is the general education teacher's way of dealing with the special education student. This is not acceptable because the BRIDGE teacher's prep period is now occupied with supervisory responsibilities that the general educator brushed off, implying all students in the school are not theirs."

Of course, the student *is* theirs—these students are on their role and assigned to them for that period. However, the mentality is, "I *let* them in my class. They are not my students, so if something comes up I don't have to deal with it, I can send them out." This is a huge barrier.

SITE COUNSELORS

Last year on Administrator 2's campus, all counselors worked with all students regardless of their level. On her current campus, one person is designated to work with the special needs population. What is good about the current arrangement is the counselor gets to know the students and is able to become familiar with their program. What is negative about the arrangement is it lends to segregation. "This is another way that these students are perceived as different and not as part of the school; 'Oh, that's Sue's student.'"

Similarly, all special needs students are sent to the same vice principal for discipline. Again, this lends to the perception that not all students belong to the school. Administrator 2 believes that if the discipline responsibilities were spread among all administrators, they would be modeling "ownership for everybody" and teacher perception would make a positive inclusive shift.

INCLUSION SUCCESSES AND CHALLENGES

On Administrators 2's campus, students are partially included. To achieve inclusion, her school has a program called AIM (Academic for Inclusion Model). This is a three-tier model. Tier one involves occasionally checking in with students to ensure all needs are being met. An example is ensuring that ramps are in good repair for an orthopedic impaired student or, if a student who has had surgery and is recovering off campus, assignments are sent home. Consultation for a student is considered a tier 1 level of support.

The second tier involves inclusion; this tier is where the majority of the students with exceptionalities are placed. With some exceptions, the usual structure includes instructional assistants being physically placed in the general education classroom if there are five or more students on IEPs. An exception to this procedure might occur if a student needs behavioral support.

The third tier consists of educating students with disabilities in resource classrooms. Some students fluctuate between different tiers. For example, a student may be tier 1 in math and tier 3 for reading. Thus, tier placement depends on a student's ability within a given subject.

Co-teaching is practiced on Administrator 2's campus, "although sadly not enough." She notes one pair of co-teachers provides seamless instruction; however, most partnerships are not so cohesive. An example of not co-teaching seamlessly would be when the content teacher is *always* at the board instructing and the special education teacher is *always* at another board writing the main points, creating a graphic organizer or is in some supportive role scaffolding for students.

"When a team lacks cohesion, it lends to the students' perception that one partner is not the 'real' teacher." Further co-teaching issues include the lack of collaboration when developing lesson plans, one teacher being absent from the room at the beginning of the class period, and only one teacher walking around to review homework. "It is tragic that both teachers are not being used to their fullest potential."

Administrator 2 elaborates that only a couple of co-teachers that teach more than one period together have a common prep time. All other co-teaching pairs are working with more than one teacher and they do not share prep with either of them. Hence, a conversation reflecting on what went well with the lesson, what could be improved or planning for the next does not happen. Therefore, the special education teacher defaults to a more supportive role. "In a perfect world, every teacher who instructs students with an IEP would have a co-teacher with a common prep time and they would be a team."

Administrator 2 notes that there are a couple of classrooms where students perceive both adults as teachers. However, without both names appearing on the students' schedules, the implication is that the second teacher is "the helper." "This is a tragedy when you look at the amount of specialized training that special education teachers go through to be 'a helper.'" Yet, with special educators floating as needed, permanently placing their name on a schedule that is in flux is not realistic.

Administrator 2 believes inclusion could be improved by making IAs co-teachers in elective classrooms and certified special educators co-teachers in content classrooms assigned to the same teacher each day. "Currently, the IAs work in the general education content classrooms and are moved around frequently." This leads to misperceptions by general educators.

One statement Administrator 2 heard a general education teacher make to an instructional aide was, "I don't need you today." Some general educators fail to understand that the IA is not in the classroom for them but rather for the students. If the lesson involves watching a video there should be a reason for watching it, a guide to follow and the IA assisting them as needed. The student's IEP states the number of hours that the student will receive support while in the general education classroom each day. IAs are not supposed to be sent away or sent out to make copies. Doing so gives the wrong impression to the student and to the classroom.

Administrator 2 provided IA training detailing their responsibilities on the first day of in-service. She told IAs, "I don't ever want to see you out getting coffee, on your cell phone, or making copies for your teacher. I don't want you to say, 'they don't need me today.' That can't happen because you are here for the student." However, she has seen IAs checking messages on their cell phones during class time; sometimes they have even left the classroom and stepped into the hallway. "This is a frustrating issue because IAs were told the expectations of their duties during their training, which began three years ago."

It is noted that general educators need to receive training regarding IA responsibilities in their classrooms. IAs feel discombobulated when the general educator instructs them to do something, such as make copies, that they were told not to do during their training. As a subordinate, they feel uncomfortable telling the teacher with whom they are placed that they are not going to do what they are told. Administrator 2 believes these issues could be mitigated if they were addressed in the teacher handbook, which is developed at each district's site.

For now, initial issues result in a conversation with the IA and follow-up occurring with the department chairs. The IA is not "called to the carpet." However, if the situation continues, Administrator 2 informs the IA they need to bring their union representative to a scheduled meeting because the conversation is going to get documented. Therefore, the nature and severity of an infraction determines the response from the administrator.

Administrator 2 muses that when she provides training to the IAs regarding not using their cell phones during the work day, the prevailing response is, "But my kids need me!" Her response is that their kids can call the school and the IA will be informed. "Having personal conversations during the professional is an unnecessary privilege."

DATA REGARDING INCLUSION

Administrator 2 states she has not seen any data which confirms that special education students' academic performance improves when they are educated with their general education peers. She speculates that one of the reasons is that the special education students are encouraged to take the alternative assessment permitted by their state, which skews the scores. "In order to know if inclusion makes a difference, then the special education students need to take the same test as the general education students. Otherwise, one is comparing apples to oranges." Administrator 2 is not aware of a consistent program currently in place that would provide the data needed to make an assertion regarding the success of inclusive programs.

Administrator 2 also does not have hard data that shows the number of discipline referrals written for special education students decreases when they are educated with their general education peers. However, she asserts that based on her collective experience, she has more behavioral issues with students segregated in special education classrooms than with students who are included. "My own perception is students do better behaviorally when they are in a general education classroom." She speculates this may be because there are more positive role models present for them, both behaviorally and academically.

THE VISION OF INCLUSION

Administrator 2 states she had no issues with inclusion at her previous school. Teachers' perceptions were the same for all students whether they were identified as being on an IEP or not. "The vision was that they were all-inclusive all the time."

As a new administrator in her current school, she has been building relationships, familiarizing herself with the school's culture and getting to know individual people and teams while developing a bond of trust. This is an important process that must occur before staff members are willing to hear her perspective. However, the issue of students on IEPs being sent back to the special education environment by general educators who teach elective courses will be addressed. "Students on a teacher's role who are included cannot be 'sent away.'"

If Administrator 2 receives information regarding a policy or procedure change specific to special education, she notifies her special education faculty via email that the issue is going to be addressed at the next department meeting, attendance required. At the meeting, she either addresses the issue herself or brings in appropriate personnel. If the information is also relevant to general educators, it is disseminated in the weekly staff meeting.

COMMUNICATION AND SUPPORT

Administrator 2 is very complimentary of the administrative team at her school. She can bring up an issue in her administrative team meeting and collectively everyone discusses the best solution, and they jointly decide how to disseminate the resulting information. Information is dispersed through staff meetings, vision teams or departments. She feels fortunate that decisions are the result of a joint effort and the administrative team is robust and collaborates frequently.

Administrator 2 supports special education teachers and IAs by fulfilling the role of an instructional leader. She views being in the classroom as a method of support. She attempts to convey the message that she is there to help; that she, the teachers and IAs are a team; and that items that need to be accomplished are not going to be merely checked off as good or bad.

If Administrator 2 has a teacher on an improvement plan, then she meets with the teacher multiple times. For example, she has reviewed one teacher's deficiencies and discussed how to remediate them as delineated in her plan. Together, they have reviewed what a model program should look like; Administrator 2 has even taken this teacher to observe several other classrooms. After their visits to the other classrooms, they sat down and mapped out ideas they observed that could be implemented immediately and other ideas that could be used in the future.

Pertinent issues have been discussed with the teacher's team to ensure they are on board. Moreover, in individual conferences, it has been emphasized that even though a remediation plan is in place, this teacher is not going to have to decipher how to address the remedial tasks without help. Everything has been done to ensure this teacher knows that she is not alone and the administrator is there to help her succeed. Thus, Administrator 2 sees herself as very supportive. She sincerely wants this teacher to be successful, which is defined as building a program that she is going to love and that is going to support her students.

The teacher is willing to hear what her administrator says, but she struggles with implementing best practices when somebody is not consistently by her side giving her prompts and praise. Administrator 2 has often had to say, "I asked you to do this by this date and it hasn't happened yet, I need it by close-of-business Monday." The teacher being reprimanded subsequently meets her deadline. Administrator 2 dislikes having to be so direct but has found it necessary. "Staying on top of issues is paramount."

Administrator 2 also recognizes that some teachers who need to be on improvement plans are not. She has reviewed some teachers' records but has not found any corrective action documented. When she observes the classroom, practices are not appropriate due to a pattern that has developed over time. "It is difficult when teachers are resistant to fulfill their professional responsibilities. Yet, it is not appropriate for the certified teacher to sit, facilitate and expect the IAs to do all of the work. Teachers need to spend time instructing kids."

Administrator 2 reiterates her willingness to help an educator succeed in whatever way she can. Her approach is to ask what is needed from her and to delineate those items on a list for the teacher and herself to reference as the year progresses. Her goal is to ensure everything is provided that the teacher needs to be successful. "I want to be sure I have always done my part." She recognizes some people don't want to "fight that battle. However, the battle isn't about the teacher, the battle is for the kids."

BENCHMARKS AND FEEDBACK

Administrator 2 does not know of any special education teacher who is involved in the creation or production of the general education assessments. She believes the special education teacher is given the assessment and takes on the responsibility of ensuring the accommodations are in place for the student after-the-fact. She feels it is unfortunate that the special educator is not involved in creating the assessments. "Being involved should occur with collaboration between the special and general educator. This strategy sets students up for success. Creating a separate test that assesses the same material for a student with disabilities is not that hard."

Administrator 2 has an open door policy for staff members and feels she is viewed as very approachable. Additionally, she is in the classroom frequently and provides feedback during or after every visit in both written and verbal form. Written feedback provides an opportunity for her to document what she sees evidence of such as engagement, congruency and response. "Written documentation provides an opportunity to provide positive, specific feedback regarding what was done well" while a verbal conversation incentivizes and motivates staff members.

Administrator 2 expounds that teachers always feel great when they get a pat on the back. "It is also great to have relationships where teachers can freely divulge strategies attempted that have been unsuccessful and to have them ask for help." This type of relationship is welcomed and not viewed as a threat by educators. Upon reflection, she believes she could refine her interactions with her four dozen IAs to complement this procedure to incentivize them.

During formal evaluations, Administrator 2 documents what the teacher did, what the students had problems with, what went well and what might be done differently. She is pleased that when she meets with her teachers many of them are often reflecting on the same questions. "Their reflections are the same or even better because they know the backstory. I love it when they are able to say what they will do differently. Sometimes I make a suggestion and they comment that they used to do what I suggested and they don't know why they stopped."

"Let's face it, virtually everything we do well that works has been stolen from someone else. I love that my suggestions are received warmly, with gratitude and are viewed as a tool and not as something condescending. It is, of course, then my job to go back in a couple of weeks to ascertain if the suggestion worked." A conversation provides incentive because the teacher knows they are going to hear from this administrator regarding specific evidence.

SPECIAL EDUCATION ACRONYMS AND ANCILLARY SERVICES

Administrator 2 does not believe her general educators know most of the special education acronyms and thinks that "they would be surprised at how much they don't know." She surmises that one strategy to open their eyes would be to provide a pretest in a staff meeting. She would then provide information electronically for them to have as a quick reference.

General educators are probably aware that speech language services are provided on campus, but they are probably not aware of occupational or physical therapists. They also have minimal awareness regarding how to support the speech language population. Conversations are not occurring between the speech language pathologists and the general education teachers to any great extent, an area that could be improved.

STANDARDIZED TESTING

Administrator 2 is not a big supporter of standardized tests. She understands that there are high stakes, stakeholders and that measurements are needed. However, they are not an adequate assessment of what students know and are able to do. She does not believe a multiple-choice test will ever be an adequate assessment. "I know for a fact that I passed tests because I was a good test taker and knew strategies for multiple-choice tests even though I had no idea what the content was." Accordingly, she knows firsthand that when she was assessed the results were not a compilation of what she knew.

An alternative state test for students with disabilities was created in her state as a way to measure what they know. But the way this test is scored is misleading as students who take the alternative test can score "advanced." Advanced on the alternative test is below basic on the regular test. Taking the alternative test means a student is far below basic to begin with, so the results are clearly skewed. "These results provide no meaningful information to parents, teachers or students."

On the other hand, if students with disabilities were to take the same test as their general education peers, they would be extremely stressed out, which isn't fair to them and could even be harmful. Yet, to exclude them is not fair either. Standardized testing can therefore be described as an exercise in futility. "It is frustrating to recognize that students on IEPs can know a lot but fail to perform well on the state standardized test because they are poor test takers."

"What special education students know is usually not being tested." Thus, the state standardized test is not an adequate measurement even though it provides statistics that interpret a basic view of everyone. Administrator 2 asserts that many colleges do not look at these test scores and not all schools include these scores on their transcripts. Moreover, her state has an exit exam which must be passed in order to graduate. Students on an IEP take this exam but are not required to pass it. "This convoluted issue of testing clearly needs to be revisited."

PARENT COMMUNICATION

Administrator 2 has no set protocol for general education teachers to communicate with parents of students with disabilities. General education teachers usually communicate with IAs and case carriers. The case carrier either reaches out to the parent or vice versa.

Most teachers would argue that they have 200 students they work with on a daily basis. Their website and student grades can be checked at any time.

Thus, if the parent has an issue they can reach out to the teacher; it is a two-way street.

PEER TUTORING

Administrator 2 states her school does not have a formal peer tutoring program. However, peer tutoring does occur in the classroom. Some students with an IEP have peer support as an accommodation. The way this is implemented is up to the classroom teacher. There is also the Helping Unite Growing Students (HUGS) Club which is not a formal program. Club members go, during Intervention, to the severely handicapped class to hang out with the students, read and play games with them.

Administrator 2 states she would love to see an elective offered for general education students who want to work with special education students. In that course they would learn about the various disabilities within special education. They would have an opportunity to work with these students as their tutors or they would run small group instruction. Additionally, teachers could utilize students from this elective class to assist in their rooms.

Several obstacles to the above idea exist. First, if students who are enrolled in a current elective chose to register in this newly created class their current class might fold due to a drop in enrollment. Second, there might not be enough students interested and those who are will not receive credit that is currently accepted by the state. Third, the good students who aspire to go to college will most likely choose more difficult coursework such as a foreign language or an advanced class to prepare them for higher education. Each of these issues needs to be addressed; a survey of interest on the campus needs to be analyzed to see if this is a worthwhile endeavor.

It is assumed that students who are already participating in the HUGS club would be interested in receiving credit. This would be doable if what they are already doing was structured and organized. In many ways, the foundation is already in place. The goal is to make the peer tutoring course academically strong so it could be accredited by the state. Then state universities would accept it as an elective high school credit.

LESSON PLANS

General education teachers have not received any specialized training regarding how to prepare lesson plans when they have students with disabilities in their classrooms. District-wide, general and special education teachers have collaborated to determine which standards are most critical in content classes. During those collaborations they talked about strategies for developing lessons considering the needs of all their students, and they did collate a binder with their ideas. However, these strategies are not specific to students with disabilities.

Many teachers use the same sheltered strategies that are used with any English language learner (ELL) for special education students. It is noted that even though all teachers have been required to receive sheltered training, they are not all utilizing the information they obtained. However, not everybody is held accountable for having these strategies in place in their room. Many teachers do not believe they need to implement the strategies because they do not have ELL students in their classroom even though they are suitable for all students.

TEACHER EVALUATIONS WITHIN INCLUSIVE SETTINGS

Teacher evaluations do not currently include items that specifically address how teachers accommodate special education students. Beginning this year, a new evaluation form is being piloted. The form is specific to the teachers' goals and essential components of instruction (ECI) strategies that are district wide.

Administrator 2 believes incorporating standards specific to working with ELL and IEP students would be a positive step. An obstacle would be that the union would not view this as helpful; rather, they would interpret it as a roadblock and contest the idea. Teachers are already getting paid less money and working with higher classroom ratios, so being "forced" to add one more thing to their plate would be considered a "negative" even though it would be good for students.

CLASSROOM ENVIRONMENT AND MANAGEMENT

Administrator 2 states training regarding how the classroom environment might accommodate students with disabilities occurs in IEP meetings and student study teams (SSTs). SST is a precursor to a student being identified as needing special education services. The SST includes an administrator, counselor, the student, the parent and teachers talking about the needs of the student, what accommodations are in place, and everything that is being done. If everything is in place and there is still a discrepancy between the student's ability and performance, then the student is recommended for testing.

Through these conversations, most teachers are aware of the accommodations that should occur in a classroom. Additionally, information regarding specific disabilities and how to address them is placed in each teacher's box. Some teachers are always willing to learn new information. Other teachers will not change what they are doing regardless of how many times they are shown what is best for students, even if it makes their life easier and mini-mizes parent complaints or concerns.

"Teachers need to understand that students on an IEP are not wired the same way as other students." For example, when all other students are plac-ing their homework in the homework basket that does not mean a student with exceptionalities is going to connect that behavior to their own need to place homework in the basket. Teachers need to implement strategies to help mitigate issues such as this. For instance, they could ask the student to put the homework in their hand or they can ask a peer to get the homework from the student. That simple step would alleviate much frustration.

General education teachers have been trained to work with learning dis-abled and emotionally disabled students via their training to work with ELL students. This is now part of their credentialing program. It is difficult to say how many teachers are actually implementing what they learned. Further-more, they are not receiving additional, ongoing training regarding differen-tiated instruction.

Monday morning late starts have changed. Originally, all teachers collab-orated during that time. This has evolved to personal time every other Mon-day. Also, the "all staff" meeting occurs only once a month because too many people cannot come after school. There was one co-lab meeting a month. The union has negotiated these valuable minutes away, which is unfortunate as those were opportunities for staff development.

Staff development days are currently furloughed due to the economic downturn. There is no opportunity for administrators to say they are going to have a breakout session regarding matters such as inclusion because they have lost full days. The consequence is that there is very little actual staff development; meetings are geared more toward strand level training and overall instructional strategies.

CREATING BUY-IN TO THE INCLUSIVE MODEL AND STRESS DUE TO ITS EXISTENCE

Administrator 2 is unsure how to create buy-in when it comes to encouraging general educators to willingly accept special education students into their classroom. Unless general educators are told they have to accept a student on an IEP into their classroom, they attempt to reject the idea. Buy-in to Admin-istrator 2 means the teacher is embracing the concept, wants it and is willing to make the IEP accommodations. "Nothing entices them to have buy-in unless it is intrinsic. Shifting that paradigm needs to occur."

Administrator 2 states her stress level is at the moderate level due to the inclusive requirement and lack of buy-in from her faculty. This is a result of having to hold extra meetings, document all contacts, create a conference summary of the meetings to properly record them, be in the classroom more, deal with the parents more and work more closely with the teachers and the IAs. Hence, more of her time is consumed simply because there is a lack of buy-in.

Administrator 2 recounted that her year began with a teacher coming to her to complain about a student with a disability being placed in her class. The teacher felt the student was incapable of doing the same quality of work that a general education student could generate. She wanted to know what to do; the teacher understood that the parent wanted the student in her class even though she was delayed. Administrator 2 responded that the student was not going to be removed from the class.

Even though having students included is more work, more "inconvenient" and they are unable to produce the same amount of work as their general education peers, the work can be modified. This allows all students to participate in a way that is meaningful to them. Grades can be modified to pass/fail if necessary. For some teachers, they feel more comfortable with this pass/fail arrangement. "But saying a student cannot do the work, does not belong in class and needs to be taken out—that is absolute exclusion and is not acceptable."

Administrator 2 has not received any specific training as a site administrator regarding inclusion, nor have any other administrators in her district. However, during the year she spent at the district office as an instructional specialist, the director of special education worked with everyone on special assignment and provided an immense amount of training. That has helped her enormously.

THE IMPACT OF THE INCLUSION MODEL

Administrator 2 believes the inclusion model positively impacts the majority of her general education students. She maintains that society underestimates the ability of general education students to accept and befriend students with special needs. She recalls a time when students who were different were beat up and bullied. General education students on her campus are comfortable with medically fragile students. They are used to students being on IEPs and do not think of them as different.

Administrator 2 ruminates that the majority of her general education teachers would *say* they embrace the inclusive model when that is not really how they *feel*. "Some do feel like inclusion is an inconvenience that adds more to their plate. But it would not be politically correct to verbalize their feelings. Inclusion does create more stress for them. They see more of the disruption to the natural flow of their class than they see a positive benefit for the few included students." On the other hand, a large number of teachers are aware that the benefits outweigh the inconvenience. "The special education teachers in particular believe this."

Although the process is far from perfect and not yet a well-oiled machine, some amazing things are happening for students with special needs at Administrator 2's site. For that she is grateful.

PACIFIC REGION TALKING POINTS

Correctly Identifying Students

- Administer a language assessment to various ethnic groups.
- Administer home language surveys.
- Implement pre-referral intervention strategies before referring a student for evaluation.
- Exit students if they no longer qualify for services.

Developing Best Practices

- Identify and utilize staff members' talents and skills.
- Provide needed supports such as interpreters, assistive technology, or training.
- Team "masters of access" with "masters of content."
- Support inclusion through collaboration among general educators, special educators, service providers and parents.
- Simple adjustments to instruction can make a big difference in results.
- Define success differently for each student.
- Place EBD students with certified, highly qualified teachers until they can demonstrate the ability to comply with school rules; then slowly transition them into general education classrooms.
- Incorporate Positive Behavioral Supports into student programming as needed.
- Visit classrooms to ensure services are delivered as intended.
- Administer and review parent surveys; address concerns as needed.
- Ensure therapists meet with teachers so they understand how a student's disability affects his or her ability to perform in the classroom.
- Expect collaboration between the special and general educator to ensure compliance with the student's IEP goals and objectives.
- Communicate with parents via email, phone calls, and websites.

Addressing Challenges to Implementing the Inclusion Model

- Attempt to schedule time for staff collaboration.

- Find ways to compensate staff for time spent addressing inclusion issues outside of their contract time.
- Employ enough ancillary staff to address the needs of the student.
- Assign paraprofessionals at the discretion of the school administrators.
- Apply for grants to fund programs.
- Determine which standards are most critical and gather curricular resources to address those standards.
- Convey all students are contemporaries in the school.
- Mitigate the perception of segregation by having all vice principals and all counselors work with all students.

Partial-Inclusion and Co-Teaching Models

- Assign counselors according to the needs of the school.
- Team teachers when one has resources needed by the other, such as lab equipment.
- Team teachers when their proximity to one another makes it prudent to do so.
- Implement the three-tiered Academic for Inclusion Model: Tier 1—Ensure the physical environment meets the needs of OI, VI, and ADHD students and consultation occurs; Tier 2—Place IAs with students on IEPs in a way that maximizes benefits; Tier 3—Provide resource classrooms for support as needed.
- Take steps to help students perceive both adults as their teachers in a co-teaching environment.
- Ensure it is understood that IAs exist for the students' benefit, not for the teachers' benefit.

Professional Development

- Bring in outside experts to train staff.
- Provide training on a continuous basis for certain subgroups of students, such as those with ADHD or on the autism spectrum disorder scale.
- Include paraprofessionals when creating the training schedule.
- Hold a leadership academy for principals during the summer so they can learn new teaching and management skills and also share solutions or ideas regarding current challenges.
- On professional training days, have break-out sessions that include inclusion training.

Staff Support

- Have an open door policy so others view you as approachable.
- Meet weekly with staff to assist and collaborate with individuals and groups as needed.
- Meet with teachers, paraprofessionals and therapists separately so they can discuss issues specific to them.
- Meet regularly as site administrators to address programmatic operational concerns or issues.
- Disseminate information through staff meetings, vision teams or departments.
- Put mechanisms into place to address issues as they occur.
- Provide refresher training; do not assume one remembers everything they were ever taught as everyone needs prompts as reminders of what they already know.
- Visit classrooms to identify patterns and ascertain what support may be needed.
- Take teachers to visit other campuses so they can learn how effective models look.
- Map ideas that can be implemented both immediately and in the future.
- Discuss pertinent issues with team members to ensure everyone is on board.
- Collaboratively generate ideas.

Special Education Terminology, Services and Strategies

- Administer an acronym pretest to staff so they realize how much they do or do not know about special education terms and processes.
- Ensure teachers are aware of basic acronyms that special educators use by providing an electronic or hard copy of terms and definitions to which they can refer.
- Provide a copy of the IEP to all teachers who work with a student with an explanation regarding the nuances of the child's disability.
- Invite therapists to speak with faculty members about the services they provide and their importance.
- Employ strategies to ensure students on IEPs meet expectations; i.e., have a peer place the homework in the basket.

Peer Tutoring

- Team general education students with their special education peers by providing opportunities to read, play games and socialize.

- Create an elective class accredited by the state so that peer tutors can earn credit.
- Train peer tutors so they understand different aspects of a disability and can better interact with the student.

Developing Lesson Plans and Assessments

- Train general educators to develop lesson plans that meet state standards and reach diverse populations.
- Place strategies in a binder for easy reference.
- Permit time for thoughtful planning that addresses the needs of inclusive classrooms.
- Develop assessments that permit included students to demonstrate knowledge in various ways—not just pen and paper.
- Hold teachers accountable—otherwise, strategies may be ignored.

Teacher Evaluations

- Consider the diverse population with which teachers work when conducting evaluations.
- Create a form that is specific to the teachers' goals and essential components of instruction strategies that are district wide.
- Incorporate standards specific to working with students on IEPs.
- Provide feedback during or after visits in both verbal and written form—verbal conversation incentivizes and motivates while written documentation provides evidence of teacher engagement, congruency and response.
- Give that much needed pat on the back.
- Reflect with the teacher when reviewing observations.

Attaining Teacher Buy-In

- Provide time for teachers to digest the need and implication of implementing inclusive strategies.
- Train teachers on the various options of assessment, including pass/fail grades when appropriate.

Chapter Three

Administrator 3: Southwest Region

Administrator 3 began his forty-one year career as a science teacher in the southwest region. After spending nineteen years in the classroom, he worked for twenty years as an administrator; ten of those were as a principal in two different high schools, which will be referred to as high school 1 and high school 2. Having also consulted for a local charter school, he is currently a district-level administrator. He asserts his past experiences give him a working concept of how to lead at this level. He describes his collective experience as "a good trip."

As a campus educator, Administrator 3 served as a science department chair for twelve years as well as on numerous committees. One noteworthy committee involved contributing to the creation of the district instructional management system that is still in place today. He has enjoyed his various positions and appreciates being able to be on various administrative teams. These positions have afforded him the ability to hire strong faculty members via the recruitment process. He has also enjoyed matching teachers' abilities with schools that can capitalize on their strengths.

CORRECTLY IDENTIFYING STUDENTS WITH DISABILITIES

Approximately 1,400 students attended high school 1; approximately 10 percent of those students were in the special education program. Approximately 2,000 students attended high school 2; approximately 9 percent of those students received special education services. Administrator 3 believes there was extensive follow-up within the school to ensure all students were correctly identified.

At high school 2, Administrator 3 does believe there were some issues with English language learners (ELL) being misidentified and placed in the special education program. He ventures that the feeder schools were not always cognizant of the appropriate process to properly distinguish between special education and ELL students. He also speculates that students were occasionally misidentified as needing special education services after entering high school.

In compliance with Child Find and to identify any student who may need additional support, a 45-day screening occurred after a student enrolled in school. The teacher, counselor or nurse evaluated the student's ability in the areas of academics, vision, hearing, adaptive, communication, social/emotional and motor skills. Occasionally, this screening led to an evaluation to determine if the student qualified for special education services.

High school 1 was elevated to the top 15 percent of schools in the state under Administrator 3's leadership. He notes the "excelling" label was attained in spite of having a large special education and ELL population. Furthermore, high school 2 improved from being ranked in the top 35 percent to the top 25 percent in the state within three years of him taking the reins. He believes if students are taught like they are meant to be, they can be successful.

Moving toward an inclusion model was a paradigm shift in how business was usually conducted. The No Child Left Behind Act (NCLB) introduced a "new wrinkle" by requiring all teachers to be highly qualified in the content they taught. Special education teachers needed to be certified in special education and highly qualified if they were the teacher of record. He does find the energy exerted "to be well worth it because students are moving forward."

Administrator 3 describes special education as unique because, while general educators teach only their content, special educators are required to be knowledgeable about and teach to all core content standards. One way this issue was addressed at high school 1 was that all department chairs would meet to discuss and review what high-performing schools were doing in the nation. They would then attempt to emulate those practices by developing similar programs, which included moving toward the inclusion model.

CHALLENGES IMPLEMENTING THE INCLUSIVE MODEL

Administrator 3 avers moving special education students into the general education environment has its challenges. Teachers need professional development to effectively work with students who have behavior needs that are consistently outside the norm. General and special educators' personalities have to be matched when co-teaching classrooms are created. Teachers have to collaboratively determine how classroom responsibilities are going to be divided; general education teachers have to recognize implementing accommodations and modifications as everyone's responsibility. All of this has to be accomplished while meeting curricular standards with a reduced budget, fewer instructional assistants and larger student to teacher ratios.

General educators were not prepared for nor did they receive any training to work with emotionally disturbed (ED) students. Furthermore, general education students were not used to being exposed to excessive amounts of inappropriate behavior in their classroom. Thus, parents would call and complain that their child's education was being interrupted because of special education students' misbehavior. It took time to educate the school community about inclusive practices.

However, Administrator 3 does not recall a general education teacher ever telling him, "I can't work with that student. Get him out of my class." He has had faculty members ask during meetings how they are going to work with behaviorally inappropriate included students. "What bothers general educators most is that they cannot discipline special education students the same way they discipline all other students. General educators feel like they have nothing to deter poor behavior and are obligated to endure the behavior of an unruly student." Taking students out of a class creates a domino effect. Administrator 3 clarifies that a great deal of attention is paid to matching students with teachers.

As an administrator, he has to determine how to best utilize professional development days. "Allocating professional time wisely throughout the course of the year is paramount." He is aware that many teachers do not feel like they are meeting the needs of all of their students. Their feeling of inadequacy is compounded by more expectations being placed upon them.

Congruent to implementing inclusion, the district developed a co-teaching model placing special and general educators in the classroom together. This model was being implemented because the No Child Left Behind Act required a content-certified educator to be the teacher of record. Being able to match co-teachers' personalities during this process was difficult.

Helping the general educator understand they had to take responsibility for determining how to meet students' needs was also challenging. Learning how to work cohesively with a co-teacher to provide appropriate accommodations was vitally important. General education teachers had to learn how not to rely solely on the special education co-teacher to implement accommodations. They also needed to understand that strategies used when implementing accommodations for the special education population are often good strategies to use with the entire population. These strategies honor the fact that all students learn at different rates.

Administrator 3 asserts the biggest challenge he has is empowering all students to meet the requirements of the regular curriculum. The pressures of tirelessly assisting students so that they can successfully pass the state standardized test their tenth grade year is immense. "The state standardized test is driving the curriculum, so if students can pass on their first opportunity, that is monumental. Not passing intensifies the pressure on everyone."

Compounding the above issue is the reality that budgets have been cut, instructional aides have been lost and student to teacher ratios have increased. Administrator 3 asserts that when budget cuts occur his district attempts to avoid affecting the classroom so as not to disturb the teachers' ability to provide quality instruction. However, this comes at the price of increasing classroom size. Currently, inclusion classroom sizes have a ratio of about 27:1; ED resource classrooms are currently about 10:1.

The departmental budget for special education is reviewed in March by his district office. This is in regards to monies spent on supplies, not for professional development. Principals (at the local level) are not involved in this process. Various departments can request workshop hours for professional development on an individual basis. The principal can support these departments by approving hours for a substitute teacher to be in the classroom. Aside from this, the district determines the budget.

"If a principal truly understands what is going on within a department via regular visits, listening to teacher concerns and providing some assistance, much dissension could be alleviated." Staff members recognize an administrator is unable to provide for everything that is requested; however, one must deliver more than lip service. If an administrator can convey that they feel their teachers' pain, their empathy goes a long way.

As teachers were in-serviced, problems began to be resolved. General educators began to develop empathy for their students. They began to understand that students with disabilities do not possess the same ability to control their behavior if they have an emotional disturbance; they might lack the social skills or mental capacity to interpret a situation or a problem the same way that their peers do.

"Implementing inclusion has been a worthwhile effort." Administrator 3 feels certain that more strategies are going to take place in his district as research regarding various models emerges. "I am sure inclusion is not the only model that is good for students." His current district is proactively seeking to understand what other models are being successfully used in schools to determine what parts can be adapted. "Self-assessment is being effected to determine if issues are being addressed in the manner hoped."

THE PARTIAL-INCLUSION AND CO-TEACHING MODELS

Administrator 3's campuses implement the partial inclusion model. As such, resource teachers are reaching out to their general education colleagues on a consultation basis. Some resource teachers are physically in the content classroom during instruction. Still others are conducting a separate resource class to support the student. The goal is to place students with disabilities in the general education environment to the greatest extent possible.

To create co-teaching teams, Administrator 3 began by in-servicing his faculty so they would understand that special needs students would be placed in their classrooms. One of the concerns general educators had was dealing with discipline within their classroom. They understood if the behavior was a manifestation of the student's disability then discipline is not administered in the same manner as it is for all other students. "Some of the teachers had a hard time accepting that."

To create teaching teams, the principal and the special education department chair worked together to determine who should be paired. Subsequently, they notified the general educator that a particular special education aide would be present in the classroom. He does not recall having any issues pairing aides with general education teachers. Thus, inclusion began with aides working with general educators; the co-teaching model (pairing two certified teachers) occurred later.

HOW EXPERIENCE EFFECTED INCLUSIVE PHILOSOPHY

Administrator 3 began his career with the philosophy that he was going to teach whatever students were given to him regardless of their strengths or abilities. His self-imposed expectation was that he was going to meet the needs of all students. Over the years, principals assigned difficult students to him, increasingly so as time transpired.

Administrator 3 had empathy for his students. He recognized they often did not have a strong support system at home (and often not at school). To help students thrive in his class or even within one subject area of his class, he wanted them to understand they have the intellect to be successful. "Once that light went on, they had some buy-in to their own education."

Upon reflection, Administrator 3 believes he was also efficacious with students because he was often their coach. Many of the students who were not doing well in class functioned well in a very structured coaching environment "because they had specific duties and timelines. Athletics is a different venue, sometimes a bit militaristic. The student does not have to raise hands, there is no checking for understanding; one simply does what needs to be done." Many students, once they understood the expectation within the structure that existed, were able to be successful.

Sometimes, the classroom is not structured in a way that the teacher is able to ascertain if everyone is getting the information needed, because certain students require more attention than others. Managing a class is an art in itself. Making sure students feel part of the class looks different for teachers than for coaches.

Players on a team have a specific assignment that they do repetitively, and the coach can oversee their performance during the entire two-hour practice. That cannot always be done in the classroom. Master teachers are very good at meeting the needs of all students, but the average teacher has trouble with moving students forward. Most teachers have to make a conscious effort to seek out struggling students and determine where they are academically challenged.

One strategy that draws students in is having conversations regarding parts of their personal lives such as how many brothers and sisters they have, what their parents do for a living or discussing other activities in which the student is involved. Administrator 3 tried to make a connection with the student by making an analogy that their success outside of the classroom could translate to their potential within the classroom. He claims, although the experience can be taxing, he really did not have a hard time working with struggling students. He believed, "If not me, who? Would I not want the same time given to my children? I always had the awareness that I had only four years to make a difference."

Administrator 3 reminisced about the summer after his third or fourth year of teaching when he was the PE teacher for students during summer school. He expresses he was very humbled during that time. He worked with students with severe needs. Some students needed their diapers changed; others needed to address their hygiene needs.

Administrator 3 was introduced to the unique world of special education. "Special education teachers face many battles on and off campus. For example, high maintenance parents want to call the shots for their child who has exceptional circumstances." Furthermore, students with severe disabilities often remain in school until they are twenty-two years of age. This means these teachers interact with those students for eight years. In many ways, the special education department is a school within a school.

His summer school experience helped him recognize that a student's home support system sometimes diverges from what educators are trying to accomplish. Lacking a solid home support system compounds what teachers are trying to do. "This was a very humbling experience for me, very humbling."

His summer school experience gave him a more global perspective regarding working with students and what they need. He realized all students want to feel like they are part of the group. As the teacher, he attempted to let them have experiences that every other student was having. When he transitioned to the world of administration, he realized he had to marry the district's and school's visions with his experiences.

"Ultimately, teachers are working with someone's child." He tried to convey to his faculty that they had the education, experiences and resources to reach students. He saw his job as providing whatever tools were needed and providing the autonomy to make decisions, thus empowering them.

Leaders need to have the mindset that it is "power with people, not power over people." Once teachers understood they had power to make decisions on their own while ensuring their administrator had a working knowledge of what was going on within their classroom, they could move forward. Administrator 3 emphasizes that being an administrator does not mean you know what is going on within your school.

"You may think you do but you do not. Sometimes teachers decide to do something their own way and they 'hide' what they are doing." He understood if he had successes with difficult children, then he could better relate to his teachers in their classrooms because of his real-life experiences. His experiences have enabled him to provide time-proven alternative strategies as suggestions.

RESOURCES

Administrator 3 believes an administrator's job is to hire quality teachers who work with students because they have a passion to do so. He considers his greatest resources to be his teachers, the experts employed at the district level, and employees at various schools. He frequently taps the knowledge possessed by various district experts. "That is why we hire them. One has to utilize all available resources; no one person has all of the answers."

Administrator 3 does not want to stifle teachers or have them think they cannot try new processes. He believes the only failure is not trying. "Teachers should have the freedom to experiment with possibilities within acceptable parameters." Everyone should be continually learning, and it should be acknowledged that mistakes will occur as they learn.

Additionally, he wants students to continue to exert themselves. "They need to understand they meet their potential when they are pressed." He is pleased that former students now tell him they felt pressured to succeed in his class, but they also understood they could do well because he maintained a positive environment and continually verbalized his belief in them.

Finding out what goes on in other schools is also a valuable resource. "Our biggest problem as educators is being unwilling to admit we do not know what to do so we try to cover our inefficiencies and deficiencies. We need to be willing to leave no stone unturned so we can reach the students. My attitude is acknowledging our way is not the only way. I believe it is incumbent upon us to seek out all possibilities."

PROFESSIONAL DEVELOPMENT

Teachers are most effective when they are given the proper tools, have the right attitude and are willing to work hard. When professional development is consistent and refined, teachers are able to move their students forward more quickly. They can identify deficiencies early, which in turn results in earlier interventions. Regular education teachers struggle with understanding how to know a student may need an intervention. If they do recognize a student is struggling, they don't always know what to do or who to reach out to for assistance.

General education teachers typically do not receive specific training regarding accommodations for students. They do, however, get information from a special education teacher regarding what can be expected from the student. Special educators, the school psychologist or the special education department chair usually provide strategies regarding what can be tried to assist the student. In most cases, the general educator reaches out to a member of the special education department if an issue arises.

At high school 1, professional development was created and provided by the curriculum instruction committee at the district office. This translated to teachers being in-serviced by experts; it also took the need for ensuring teachers receive professional development off of the administrators' plates. Principals were subsequently informed about the training so when they entered a classroom they could see if the strategies taught were being implemented.

"Principals do not always have the expertise of knowing all aspects of a certain course, so it is reasonable to rely on experts. What principals can do is follow through by ensuring teachers are doing what they say and by keeping data to see if it is making a difference." Administrator 3 regularly revisited his teachers' program improvement plans. At the end of the first grading period he was able to inquire, "Here is what you said you were going to do. Are you doing what you said? If not, why not? Is it making a difference? Has anything changed?"

The program improvement plan is a working document that should be changing all the time. "Planning is fluid and should change as information warrants. Students change and plans should reflect those changes. Populations vary and so they need to be worked with in different ways."

Administrator 3 posits that principals should collaborate with their teachers during faculty meetings. They need to ask, "What are your difficulties? In what areas do you need help?" Principal also need to rely on their department chairs and the experts at the district office. "Failing to do so is shameful. A conscious effort needs to be made to stay in touch with issues. Otherwise, there is the attitude if it isn't addressed, then it doesn't exist."

"Just because a principal is not hearing about problems, it does not mean everything is going well. In the end, good instruction translates into good scores. Principals therefore need to make sure their teachers have the tools necessary to provide good instruction."

Administrator 3 never received any specific training to learn how he, as an administrator, could successfully lead his campus to implement the inclusion model. As a principal, the special education director informed him about the training his teachers were receiving and how their training was expected to look. However, as far as professional development goes, that did not occur for him.

DATA

Administrator 3 has not seen any specific data regarding the impact inclusion has for the special education student. However, the end result of passing the state standardized test has been favorable. He notes that special education students at high school 2 made vast improvements under the partial inclusion model. "The proof of the pudding was the success of the special education students as evidenced by their passing the mandated tests. That was the result of the team being on the same page." Administrator 3 reiterates having the right people in a position that plays to their strengths is imperative.

Administrator 3 does not believe placing students with special needs in the same classroom as their general education peers prevents the regular education student from progressing. He does not know if inclusion has a positive impact on the general education students academically, but he does believe inclusion helps them grow socially. Being able to interact is good for the special needs students to not be sheltered from the normal expectations.

"Everyone is going to have to be able to function in society and it is only appropriate that we help them reach their greatest potential." In an inclusive environment, students with disabilities are not only learning core course content, they are learning valuable coping skills, behavioral and academic strategies, and how to think using higher level processes. This may not be at the same level as the general education students, but if they were not included they may not be as well prepared as they otherwise are.

The only data Administrator 3 has to substantiate his above statement is what he has observed. "Classes operate normally, there are few disruptions, and students are progressing and are well-adjusted." Measuring the success of an inclusion model goes beyond test scores. Relying on his experience as a teacher and as an administrator, "I can absolutely say that inclusion has made a big difference."

Regarding behavior, Administrator 3 discussed discipline referrals as they relate to a student's disability. "ED students often act out regardless of their environment. In-servicing teachers and providing them with strategies helps mitigate discipline referrals." Administrator 3 states he often became the personal disciplinarian for the special education department.

As schools have moved toward an inclusion model, he has noted a positive trend. Teachers frequently confer with students regarding their behavior instead of relying on administrators to oversee discipline. He has overheard teachers chide their students, "You never acted this way before; I am disappointed that you are disrupting class now." The student sees their teachers as someone who cares about them and not as adversaries.

Eventually, all teachers started taking ownership of all students. They gained a greater appreciation for students who had different abilities that are often taken for granted. The payoff with included students was a more immediate feeling of gratification, "because students with special needs tend to respond more readily than their general education peers. Often, general education students don't visibly change for four to five years." Conversely, special education students often show their gratification in four to five days. Experiencing a more immediate payoff was a unique experience for general educators.

STANDARDIZED TESTS

Regarding standardized tests, Administrator 3 understands baseline data is needed before one can show that there is improvement. "Standardized testing does that; the issue is it is not the only means of determining how successful a student or a school is. There has to be other avenues of determining success other than this data."

"Unfortunately, education has become the whipping boy of the nation's woes. Society places all of the country's woes on our teachers saying they aren't prepared and aren't teaching our kids. This presents a lot of pressure." Administrator 3 submits that there must be other ways besides standardized tests to show student progress. A student may not be at grade level but may have made significant progress. "We all believe all kids can learn, but we have to acknowledge that they all learn at different levels and at different rates."

Administrator 3 believes student improvement should be viewed as a continuous process. He is distraught that excelling students can move from an affluent community to a poorer district and not receive an education at their ability level. "In this situation, educators are not doing a service to the student. Taking advantage of what a student already knows and taking him to the next level is vital. A student should enter society as well prepared as possible whether gifted or severely disabled."

One way a student can enter society well prepared is by connecting with one or two teachers. This often propels them to have a successful, productive adult life. Additionally, connecting a student with technology prepares them for today's world. Students need to have the ability to perform basic math, reading and writing skills and technology is one avenue in which this can be accomplished.

Similarly, businesses that will be demanding technological knowledge need to provide schools with money so they can obtain technology for today's youth. Tax dollars are not enough to help schools keep up with technology because it evolves so rapidly. There should be a marriage with industry and education to fill the gaps.

There is a job for everybody out there; everyone has a special need or niche that they can fill. The sad piece occurs when there is a student who has not been made aware of his full potential. Obtaining a diploma should be a real accomplishment. It should demand effort that pays dividends because the student worked hard and indicated they could meet demands.

There has been talk about having various diplomas; the con to this approach is creating a class society. Success should be measured by what one gives back to society. That is what has made us great as a nation. Giving back ensures we stay on the right path.

SCHOOL PROGRAMMING

The school psychologist in Administrator 3's district collaborates with the special education department head to monitor the students' four year plan. Currently, counselors in his district have over 400 students assigned to them. Dedicating one counselor to the special education department only would mean the other counselors have even more students; this would clearly create problems. He believes training all counselors regarding the unique needs of the special education student is more beneficial than having only one dedicated counselor knowledgeable about this population.

Administrator 3 believes the best use of instructional aides depends on where the need lies. Communicating with the special education department chair helps facilitate this process. Special education teachers need to remain in regular contact with the general education teacher to ensure instructional aides are in the classrooms where student support is most needed. All teachers need to recognize the assignment of aides is a fluid process.

General education teachers should feel comfortable with having aides in their classroom. Aides must have an associate's degree, or they must have completed sixty hours of coursework or they must pass the paraprofessional test. The test demonstrates the aide's ability to assist with reading, writing

and math instruction. The special education department chair should careful-
ly screen potential matches to partner within classrooms.

The overall day-to-day business of deciding where an aide should be
placed occurs when there is a good working relationship with the special
education department. Special educators need to ask how they can support
general educators as they work with special education students. Likewise,
general educators need to verbalize what they need the special education
teacher to provide as support or accommodations.

In other words, both teachers should ask how they can help and state what
they need. "If students could see that their teachers have identified a deficien-
cy that is being collaboratively addressed, whether academic or social, it
would be beneficial. This may exist to some extent, but it would behoove us
to implement the strategy on a regular basis."

STAFF SUPPORT

Administrator 3 has an open door policy. He recalls that when he became
principal, his former colleagues did not feel comfortable approaching him
even though they knew him. He had to break down the walls that existed.
Eventually, his teachers learned they could confide in him.

As a principal, he instructed his vice principals to share information
teachers had confided in them with him. However, he made it clear this was
not a two-way street. In other words, "the buck stopped with me." Therefore,
he was to be made aware of all information, but he was only going to divulge
what he knew with his vice principals on a need-to-know basis.

Administrator 3 believes as long as teachers know their principal is there
for them and will provide opportunities for them, "that knowledge goes a
long way." He always wanted his teachers to know that he would provide a
united front with them when working with the parent. He acknowledges it
takes a period of time to gain trust and some teachers never do trust their
principal. "Teachers know when communication is not sincere. If they reach
out to their principal and the principal drops what he is doing to address their
concerns, then the teacher feels valued and will work harder."

SPECIAL EDUCATION TERMINOLOGY, SERVICES AND
STRATEGIES

Administrator 3 believes it is a good practice for general educators to understand special education acronyms. Acronyms and terminology have value
when a general educator observes how the "label" is manifested within the
student. Additionally, the general educator can then participate more intelli-
gently in an IEP meeting because the specific needs and goals noted on the

IEP can be addressed. Interestingly, many general educators believe needing to know about acronyms and the disabilities with which they relate "is just one more thing on my plate."

General educators often do not relate to special education issues; having to learn about them is viewed as burdensome. However, once teachers implement strategies for their special education students and see that those strategies also work well with the regular education students, they are more willing to utilize them. If implementing something new is put in the context of "it's a good learning strategy regarding all students," then they seem to be more accepting of it as a valuable tool that is available to them.

Supporting teachers looks different in an ideal world than in reality. The pressures on the classroom teachers are phenomenal. Every time they turn around they are told about one more thing they have to do. What they want is to just be able to teach their content. In today's world, it is never going to be like that.

It is difficult to get teachers to understand "these are our kids." Moving students forward should be the collective effort of the school via the individual departments. Students are not just "yours" and "mine." Using best practices from each other helps us move to a higher level. It is interesting that, when a teacher does something well, they don't want to share that strategy with everyone else.

Administrator 3 recalls a time he worked for a business that implemented the effective strategy of regularly sharing their successes. No one kept secrets. The company understood that once an individual shared their secret of success with everyone else, not only would that individual become more successful but the organization would grow. Other employees would implement the same strategy and in turn attain success. Likewise, within the school environment if individual teachers share their success, then the whole department will move forward because all of the students can be successful.

Achieving more team teaching and having more common periods to do common preps would be beneficial. However, schedules prevent this from happening. Currently, common prep time often occurs after school when everyone is tired. There is no time before school because teachers are preparing for their day.

Teachers are in the trenches every day. "As an administrator, I take my hat off to them. I do everything I can to support the classroom teacher." Teachers provide a service, even those with difficult personalities. It is incumbent upon the administrator to separate a teacher's personal attitude from the teacher's professional ability. Some individuals may get under an administrator's skin but still have the ability to produce successful students.

Administrator 3 believes the more information a general educator has regarding a student's disability, the better prepared that teacher is to successfully provide guidance. Therefore, knowing if a student is receiving speech language, occupational or physical therapy is necessary. He recalls that when he was a teacher, the more knowledge he possessed the better equipped he was to work with troubled students.

"Understanding what a student is going through helps the teacher have empathy. Students know when they are perceived as a nuisance or an inconvenience; they are sensitive. Having information about students helps the teacher know how to best reach them."

PEER TUTORING

Administrator 3 asserts that peer tutoring is one of the ways teachers can meet the needs of all students. In high school 1, students could enroll in a peer tutoring course during the summer. They were trained regarding strategies to remediate struggling students. During the school year they were assigned to a specific classroom, usually math or English, during a specific period and earned one course credit. Examples of content needing remediation include composition writing, writing persuasive essays and other areas of the tutors' strength.

Moreover, teachers implemented a peer tutoring system within their classroom. If one student was exceptionally strong in a specific subject area, that student might work individually with a struggling student while the teacher reviewed for a test with the rest of the class. Administrator 3 believes this is an acceptable practice if parameters are established.

For example, the teacher needs to ensure tutoring is indeed occurring and needs to make sure neither student misses important instruction. The goal is for the tutee to make progress. Additionally, the peer tutor should be able to convey to the teacher areas in which the tutee has made gains or remains deficient. This permits the teacher to focus on the specific needs of the student that might have otherwise been neglected. Teachers should use this strategy on a regular basis to capitalize on a student's full potential.

This strategy can also be used in specialty classes. Administrator 3 expresses his surprise at the empathy general education students have that supersedes the adults'. The tutors have a natural connection with their fellow students that teachers are sometimes lacking in spite of their excellent abilities as educators. Administrator 3 notes that peer tutoring would be an excellent strategy to implement in resource classes. Starting this process at the high school level might be an avenue through which prospective teachers can be channeled.

CREATING LESSON PLANS FOR INCLUSIVE CLASSROOMS

Administrator 3 is not aware of any specific professional development that is occurring in his district to help general education teachers develop lesson plans to specifically help students with special needs. He asserts that master teachers would be developing these plans naturally. They already have their classes broken down to levels based on a student's current knowledge base. They know the needs of the student and do this on a regular basis.

Most teachers, however, would be resistant to being told they need to attend yet another training class. "A better strategy would be to ask teachers what they are doing in the classroom that is helping special education students be successful. Presenting needed information in this format to the faculty would be more palatable." This would help break the mentality that they are being told what to do. They would see it as somebody trying to give them meaningful information.

Teachers need to understand they have to meet the needs of all students. This is the law. In the future, both general and special education students will coexist in the classroom. Knowing how to present information on a broad scale is crucial.

TEACHER EVALUATIONS

Teachers are not being evaluated differently than they were prior to the push for inclusion. Principals are still looking at the level of instruction and how effective that instruction is. They want to know if teachers are consistently checking for understanding, if there is student engagement and if teachers are assessing their students. "We must meet all of the needs of all of the students within the classroom."

Now that test scores are part of a teacher's evaluation, different students' needs must be addressed. Because teachers are being held accountable, they need to be given more information through professional development. The question is how they should navigate lesson plan development; should they develop a separate lesson plan for students with special needs or can they creatively adapt a single lesson plan for all students? Ultimately, if students' scores are poor, that reflects poor teaching.

ATTAINING TEACHER BUY-IN TO THE INCLUSION MODEL

Administrator 3 believes including teachers from the ground up regarding what is about to happen and giving them the opportunity to have input is crucial to attaining buy-in. Preconceived notions need to be dispelled. One way to do this is to bring in teachers from other schools who have implemented inclusion so they can discuss what they are doing to help all students be successful. Laying groundwork ahead of time releases the fear of the unknown.

Some schools pilot programs before the program is widely implemented. Sometimes teachers go to their principals and disclose what they want to try. (The principal should run the idea by district office for approval.) Sometimes teachers request time to visit other schools to see what a program looks like. This dispels myths and provides insight.

When teachers know that their concerns are taken seriously and the administrator wants them to be comfortable, they internalize that as receiving the help they desire. When teachers visit other schools, they usually learn that their fears are unfounded. They often become champion teachers who request more of what they originally feared; in this case, more students with special needs.

Administrator 3 states working with students with special needs was quite stressful in the beginning. Many students were not identified within the full realm of their disability. For example, teachers often knew a student had a learning disability but did not know that a student had ADHD. Therefore, how to provide the support needed was not fully known. As a teacher himself, he felt he effectively worked with special education students and believed he could make a difference with them.

THE COMMON CORE PROGRAM

Administrator 3 states his current pressure is meeting the obligations required by the Common Core program. Common Core State Standards were developed to offer a reliable, clear understanding of what students are expected to learn so teachers and parents know what they need to do to help them. The standards are designed to be robust and relevant to the real world, reflecting the knowledge and skills students need for success in college and careers and to compete successfully in the global economy.

Common Core is locally described as a design-down, teach-up program. Administrator 3's district is stressing literacy and application synthesis. The Common Core assessment is not the general knowledge regurgitation test that many claim the state standardized test to be. Literacy is emphasized; within the math department, this translates to analyzing equations.

"Several years ago, teachers were free to teach content they knew, not just content in which they were certified. This evolved to developing a curriculum that was going to be taught in every school. Then this progressed to teaching subject matter at the same pace and testing on the same day."

Teachers are now limited to teaching only courses in which they have obtained certification. The country established national standards per NCLB in 2001 that left evaluation to the states. Now a national curriculum called Common Core Curriculum has been developed. There is a thirty-four-state consortium and an online test that must be passed for a student to graduate. This requires every school to have enough computers for all students to test on the same day.

Special education is definitely going to be affected by Common Core requirements. Students are going to be required to pass the test. Nobody knows what this is going to look like. Educators are asking how preparing students is going to be accomplished.

Administrator 3 maintains that "Good teaching is going to accomplish much no matter what the curriculum is. Teachers convey meaningful information and test the material they deliver. When students pass their test it demonstrates they learned what they were taught. An evaluation is based on the curriculum."

Similarly, good teachers should be able to provide enrichment. "There is room for teaching required material and for including enrichment. Good teachers manage their lesson plans so enrichment, about 10 minutes during a lesson, can be provided." Enrichment exposes students to additional information while not holding them accountable for it on a test.

STRESS

Teachers are stressed regarding the new Common Core requirements. This stress, in turn, affects their ability to operate optimally on a daily basis. Likewise, this stresses Administrator 3 because he wants to be able to support his teachers by meeting their needs and providing reassurance that they can succeed. He understands sometimes a seed is planted that blooms at some point in the future.

Administrator 3 ruminates that sometimes policies are created and implemented that are not always in the best interest of the student. There are budgetary issues and different agendas. His agenda is to provide the best quality education regardless of funding. His passion is pure and consistent. He does not worry about himself; rather, he worries about new teachers who often do not remain in education.

There are many demands within special education. Many adults do not want to get involved in education because of the plethora of laws and federal regulations. Keeping up with IEPs and the threat of lawsuits brought by parents is a deterrent. Expectations are only intensifying. It is stressful knowing good people are avoiding education as a career because it is viewed as a thankless job. Encouragingly, once someone begins their career as a teacher they often feel rewarded.

Administrator 3's district recently held an aspiring administrator's workshop. Real-life stressful situations were presented. One of the goals was to emphasize both administrators and teachers are congruently in the business of educating students. The weight of meeting everybody's expectations is shared. "Students on campus belong to everybody. Too many teachers view themselves as individuals working alone."

INCLUSION'S IMPACT

Administrator 3 believes that inclusive practices that he implemented on his campuses have had a positive impact on students with disabilities. He acknowledges his teachers may not agree because they do not have the perspective that an administrator has. He also believes general education students have benefitted by learning acceptance, tolerance and social values.

General education students learn to understand that everyone is unique and possesses different abilities. Students learn they are endowed with certain abilities; some people have more ability in certain areas while others have less ability. Yet, we are all valuable people.

General education teachers usually view inclusion as one more thing on their plate. However, after working in an inclusive environment for about a year, they tend to see the value in the program because they see the growth of the student and the impact they had as a teacher. Graduation is often a time teachers realize the fruits of their labor and the value of their efforts. The end of the year is the time they realize their progress. Thus, appreciation for inclusion occurs "down the road."

On one hand, inclusion has taken some of the work away from special education teachers as they are not located only in resource classrooms. Conversely, inclusion has provided more work for special educators because their general education colleagues are requesting more help to work with students with special needs. Having to meet the needs of multiple adults, some of who are very needy, can be challenging. Nevertheless, not being the sole person responsible for the students' education is a positive.

Inclusion enables special education teachers to have more opportunities to interact with their general education colleagues because they are not relegated to work only in their segregated resource environment. They have time to reach out to their colleagues and utilize their energies and talents to a greater capacity. For example, they can physically assist in the general education classroom or work with a general educator on a consultation basis.

This is important because special educators often do not feel like they are part of the campus faculty. Yet, it should be recognized that having to reach out to multiple teachers could be viewed as "One more thing I have to do.

However, seeing their students being successful as an end result should be inspiring."

CONCLUSION

Administrator 3 concludes by saying he must now focus on understanding how Common Core affects special education in and out of the inclusive environment. He ponders how the role of the special educator is going to change. "The requirements are going to be more demanding and labor-intensive regarding higher-level thinking skills, literacy skills, and cognition." Tests are going to change and he wonders what that is going to look like for the special education student and teacher. He believes this is going to be a significant issue.

Administrator 3 fears that initial testing will result in low test scores because of the requirements "that no one yet has a handle on." He wonders if the finances are available to meet the professional development needs that should occur to support teachers and students regarding this matter. The district office has to determine how their money and energy is going to be spent. Special education needs to be included in this decision-making process.

Special education teachers have a certain methodology that allows them to influence and bond with students in their classrooms; these teachers' talents must be fully maximized. This can be accomplished by general educators capitalizing on the knowledge their special education colleagues possess. In the end, all good general and special education teachers use accommodations, modifications and sheltered English immersion strategies for their students because they are sound.

"My vision has not changed. As the principal and instructional leader of my school, I have always wanted to provide our students with the best education possible. When students receive their diploma, they should feel confident that they have an edge over any other schools' students. My goal is for my graduates to be sought after by employers and to be highly equipped to continue their education in the post-secondary environment."

"When a student has my name on their diploma, they can be assured that I have given them my all. I want my students to have a better house than I have, a better car than I have, make more money than I make, provide for their families in ways that I could not provide for my family and I want them to give back more to society more than I could ever dream of. That is my vision and hope for our students."

SOUTHWEST REGION TALKING POINTS

Correctly Identifying Students with Disabilities

- Comply with the Child Find Law and conduct a forty-five-day screening after a student registers.

Developing Best Practices

- Research the practices of successful schools and emulate them.
- Implement self-assessments to determine if issues are being addressed in the manner hoped.
- Hire quality teachers; they are your greatest resource.
- Tap the knowledge possessed by experts.
- Allow teachers to try new strategies within acceptable parameters.
- Admit you do not know what to do if you need help.
- Collaborate with teachers during faculty meetings.
- Make a conscious effort to stay in touch with the issues.
- Encourage ownership.

Addressing Challenges to Implementing the Inclusion Model

- Provide professional development to address strategies for working with students with emotional behavior disorders.
- Determine how to best utilize professional development days.
- Create a budget that permits teachers to provide quality instruction.
- Listen to teachers' concerns and attempt to provide assistance or relief; even if you cannot, the fact you listened and tried carries much weight.
- Ensure teachers have consistent collaboration time.

Partial-Inclusion and Co-Teaching Models

- In-service faculty prior to implementing inclusion.
- Provide avenues for general educators to learn how to honor different learning styles and rates of retention of their students.
- Match general and special educators' personalities when creating co-teaching teams.
- Permit co-teaching teams to collaboratively determine how classroom responsibilities will be divided.
- Keep co-teaching classroom ratios 1:3; for example, ten special education students in a classroom of thirty total students.

- Encourage resource teachers to reach out to their general education colleagues.
- Attempt to schedule common preps.

Professional Development

- Consistently schedule meaningful professional development.
- Ensure experts train teachers.
- Become informed and support the training that teachers received.

Using Data and Standardized Tests

- Pay attention to trends.
- Use data as a baseline so you will know if your students are improving.
- Remember standardized tests are not the only means of determining success.

Staff Support

- Have an open door policy.
- Ensure vice principals communicate confidential information to the principal so he or she is in the loop.
- Present a united front when working with parents.
- Encourage teachers to share their successes so everyone can learn and grow.

Special Education Terminology, Services and Strategies

- Ensure general educators understand how a student's label is manifested within the student.
- Inform general educators about common special education acronyms.
- Discuss accommodations as a valuable strategy for all students.
- Stress all students are "ours."
- Ensure general education teachers know if a student is receiving ancillary services and how the need for the service impacts the student's abilities.

Peer Tutoring

- Train peer tutors to understand strategies to remediate struggling students.
- Assign peer tutors to their tutee according to their strengths.
- Encourage teachers to informally match a strong student to one who struggles during test reviews.

- Ensure peer tutors who are class members do not miss valuable instruction.
- Verify the tutor can convey to the classroom teacher areas in which the tutee is deficient.

Developing Lesson Plans

- Have one or two teachers state a successful strategy being used to create lesson plans that addresses the needs of diverse populations.

Teacher Evaluations

- Look at the level of instruction and determine if it is effective.
- Ensure teachers are consistently checking for understanding.
- Determine if there is student engagement.
- Consider the scope of student assessment.

Attaining Teacher Buy-In

- Include teachers' input from the ground up.
- Bring in teachers from other schools who have implemented inclusion to describe what they are doing and what works.
- Lay groundwork before implementation.
- Provide time for teachers to internalize the process.
- Permit teachers to visit other schools so they can observe inclusive classrooms.

Chapter Four

Administrators 4 and 5: Rocky Mountain Region

Education is a second career for Administrator 4. His bachelor's degree is in pre-law and his master's degree is in education administration. He has taught English, geography, speech, American government and study skills. Additionally, he has been an athletic director as well as a football and basketball coach. Administrator 4 has been an administrator for nineteen of the twenty-three years he has been in education; seventeen of those years have been in his current district where he initially wore two hats for six years as both assistant principal and teacher. Subsequently he was the special education director and elementary principal for one year. He began his twelfth year as superintendent and secondary principal. Currently he wears three hats as the superintendent, secondary principal and a teacher at his rural district in the Rocky Mountain region.

Administrator 5 is the district special education and Title I director as well as a school principal, testing coordinator and teacher in the same district as Administrator 4. An educator for twenty-four years, she has been in her current district for nine years. She taught third grade for three years and has been an administrator for twenty-one years. Her bachelor's degree is in elementary education with a special education minor, and her master's degree is in education leadership, principal K–12 with a special education director endorsement. Lastly, she has an education specialist degree for her superintendent endorsement.

A significant shift in demographics has occurred in Administrators 4 and 5's district due to the downsizing of the main employer, the government. This has resulted in the district having a very small tax base to support the needs of the school. Since the state has moved school funding from property tax to sales tax, all of the district's support comes from the state. When the recession hit, state funds to support the school were greatly reduced.

In 2008 resources peaked; since that time approximately 20 to 25 percent of the funds to purchase resources have been lost. Subsequently, 75 percent of the state's school districts have shifted to supplemental levies—local property tax levies that replace money lost from the state. However, Administrators 4 and 5's district has such a small tax base that they do not have the ability to get a levy passed. Because the cost of utilities, supplies, benefits and bussing is not diminished when resources are lost, the result is a need to cut personnel. Reduction in force (Riffing) of classified staff therefore ensued.

Approximately 13 percent of the students are on individual education plans (IEPs) in this Rocky Mountain district. Administrator 4 notes in the last 2–3 years about two-thirds of the students who have entered the district are high needs; 45 percent have been in special education with the other 21 percent being general education students who are 2–3 years behind their peers. The rapid change in demographics and the lack of resources have combined to have a significant impact on student scores. Administrator 5 laments that when it comes to high stakes testing, one student in a small class who has a low score has a significant impact on the class average.

Administrator 4 began his education career teaching four years at a middle school in a larger district than where he currently works. Approximately 1,300 students were attending a school that was built for 800 students. Students on IEPs were taught in a resource pullout environment that consisted of twenty-five students per classroom. Students rotated out of Administrator 4's classroom per their individual schedule. In fact, he had very little contact with these students.

As a new teacher, he had no thoughts about the students' programming because he was too new to education. He realized students were missing his content but he also realized they needed help in their area of disability. Thus, he did not process student programming as right or wrong, "it's just the way it was—it's what I walked into." When he moved to his current district, its small size made it more intimate; teachers were able to get to know their students better.

Administrator 4 states his educational law class was what clued him into who special education students were, what to do (or not do), and what IEPs were all about. Otherwise he does not remember any specific class that discussed special educational issues or needs. Conversely, Administrator 5 initially learned about students with disabilities through the special education classes she took to obtain her minor degree and again when she acquired her certification as a special education director. However, the information received when obtaining her undergraduate degree was admittedly minimal. Both conclude that most administrators are not equipped to work optimally with the special needs population. If a small district does not have someone on staff with Administrator 5's knowledge, skills and abilities, administrators must rely on their special educators' abilities and willingness to conform to the law.

Administrator 4 submits administrators must learn their responsibilities quickly while on the job; learning that best prepares one to be an effective leader does not take place in the classroom. Attending educational law seminars that review legal mandates are helpful as approximately 25 percent of the discussion is relevant to special education. He is proud that his district has never been sued during his leadership and proclaims this is a result of learning from his bad experiences with parents or teachers. "I used those situations as 'teachable moments.'" Ultimately, experience enables one to improve and learn how to interact constructively with distraught parents and overwhelmed teachers. Yet, nothing can prepare an administrator for every scenario that will occur during his tenure.

Administrator 5 has worked in small districts her entire education career. When she taught third grade, she worked with students who were on IEPs. These students, who were mostly learning disabled (LD), were never out of the general education classroom for more than a half hour per day. When they did leave, it was during times that it did not affect the content work in their classroom. Moreover, general educators worked closely with the special educator to modify lessons and ensure students on IEPs were receiving appropriate instruction.

She has tried to continue that process in her current school district. Students may be in resource two hours per day because they are cognitively impaired (CI), but this usually does not occur all at one time and consideration is given to students being in content classes as appropriate. However, the lack of personnel is affecting scheduling and the ability to provide side-by-side instruction. General educators in the elementary setting are fairly good at providing differentiated instruction and utilizing accommodations; however, this does not mean all of them are good at this process. A few teachers still hold the viewpoint that, "This is not my job."

Administrator 4 adds that the district just lost their long-term elementary special education teacher of thirty-four years. This caused moments of panic and doubt that the position was going to be filled because special education positions are difficult to fill, especially in a rural area that is isolated and that provides little incentive to inspire potential applicants. After weeks of advertising the position, a special education teacher who had previously taught in the district returned to the area and applied. Mercifully, this teacher is also a psychologist and will be able to do testing, "which is a godsend for us."

Also, a secondary teacher was relieved from her position due to a lack of performance. Fortunately, a young person took the position; unfortunately, he lacked the essential characteristics and skills required to fulfill his obligations. "It is difficult to find quality people who are willing to go to rural environments." Administrator 4 has found that many recent teacher graduates do not seem to be leaving the universities with training that is appropriately preparing them to work in classrooms as the teacher of record. It's very difficult for anyone new to the field of education to possess all of the skills they are ultimately going to need. Furthermore, in rural schools, teachers must often prepare lesson plans for multiple subjects. Subsequently, these teachers need a lot of support; for special educators, the work load is double due to the paperwork.

Administrator 5 feels one of the reasons teachers appear unprepared is that they don't fully understand the composite of special education students. Students with disabilities are academically behind their peers and need additional supports such as modified or differentiated instruction. However, the new teacher is overwhelmed with a classroom full of diverse students who need layered lesson plans that must be prepared without supervision. A student who may need to be referred for testing is not because the teacher feels quashed. She asserts that one way her district alleviates this situation is by providing all new teachers with a mentor at their grade level or in their content area during their first year in the district.

Also, response to intervention (RTI) training and practices are in place. Title I staff, described as an amazing group, work with small groups in the classroom to help students increase their skill level. However, both certified and classified staff members require additional training to better understand special education students and the reason they might not be on task. Too often their lack of performance is mistakenly considered to be an attitude of rudeness or defiance instead of a result of their biological or neurological makeup. Some teachers do not care to learn about different students' exceptionalities, for example those with Asperger's syndrome, who may need different treatment in terms of discipline or scheduling because of their disability. Many teachers want the situation to be more black and white, which it is not.

At the elementary level, IEP training occurs at the beginning of every school year. Students who are on IEPs are discussed and the complete IEPs are given to the students' teachers. Furthermore, the accommodation page is extracted for teachers to place in their plan books and files for substitute teachers. The importance of accommodations are stressed, especially the fact that they are a legal requirement.

In the spring teachers who are currently working with a student on an IEP meet with receiving teachers to discuss specific strategies that do and do not work for the student. When the school year begins, the teacher receives an additional copy of the accommodations that describe if the child can, for example, have modified assignments, stand up beside his desk, walk around the room or have a specific cue that indicates he can leave for a pre-designated area. In brief, teachers are informed of a student's needs well in advance of receiving the child.

At the high school level, teachers attend IEP meetings. When the new school year begins, every student's IEP is discussed with all of the teachers so every teacher is well aware of each student's needs. The special educator at the high school prints the accommodation page for every teacher so that it can be placed in their plan and substitute book. This simple process mitigates the need for general educators to plod through a twelve-page document to determine what the accommodations are.

Administrator 4 emphasizes that substitute teachers need to be well informed of every student's accommodation. This is very important because, if the substitute teacher does not have knowledge of a specific student's needs, "the substitute might come unhinged on a specific student. We have run into these problems in the past and are proactively trying to address them. However, sometimes the substitute teacher does not read their file or the teacher forgets to include the accommodation page in the substitute packet." Administrator 5 projects that an additional support for general educators would be to provide a list of specific disabilities with detailed descriptions of their characteristics.

CHALLENGES AND SOLUTIONS

Administrator 4 stresses that today's teachers are asked to perform miracles. "It is as if they are being blasted with information from a fire hose." This includes the expectation to implement RTI, plan lessons, attend meetings, understand school methods and meet the accountability system. When a high needs student enters the classroom after school has been in session for six weeks, teachers understandably feel like a monkey wrench has been thrown in the mix. Meeting all of the demands of every student is difficult and frustrating, especially with a revolving door.

Excellent, experienced teachers understand how to accommodate students both academically and socio-emotionally. Others are not willing to dedicate themselves to the extent necessary that permits the student to succeed, which in turn requires the administrator to constantly prod the reluctant teacher. There are universal issues involved in working with students on IEPs including understanding that every time a student acts out or is struggling with their work the teacher cannot send them out of the classroom to the special educator. Some teachers don't care enough to go the extra mile no matter what assistance an administrator provides. Other teachers give 110 percent to every child.

When Administrator 4 talks to his teachers, he underscores that his responsibility to the district is to reduce risk. Failure to follow an IEP puts the district at risk for being sued. He emphasizes that accommodations are not options, they are legal requirements. "We are bound to do them, these are not optional and you can't pick and choose which ones you want to do. If it's in the IEP, you better be doing it. You may not be perfect but you better be giving an effort. Ignoring them may be okay for you, but it's not okay for the district or for the student."

Administrator 4 bemoans the fact that the budget drives a lot of decisions and experiences that occur within a school. As was true for so many other districts, teacher benefits were cut for the 2012–2013 school year and they did not receive a raise. Furthermore, teachers received furlough days that had been designated as professional development days. While the staff was happy to have days off, it came at the price of their training and collaboration time being eliminated. "It's hard to complete your mission when you don't have the resources or time. The staff resents years of their benefits and pay being reduced and it also makes it difficult to do one's mission well."

Surrounding districts that are the same size as Administrators 4 and 5's district have more money because of the property and tax base. "It's amazing what they can obtain that we can't. However, we are a top performing school." The question remains how one improves when they are already at the top of the academic scale, a requirement presently mandated by No Child Left Behind. The current system is set up to reward those who show improvement, not those who are already excelling. "Administrator 5 is unfairly penalized because she has already reached the top and cannot show any growth. The only way to show growth at this point is to get knocked down so she can once again improve. This may change when the system transitions to the Common Core State Standards."

Administrator 4 is concerned because his district is rated at the top level in his state. He fears the legislature is going to say they don't need money because they are performing well in spite of the fact their budget has been cut 20 percent. Responding that teachers are leaving the profession, or educators are leaving the state so they can get paid more money or arguing that persuading good teachers to come to a rural area is difficult seems to be a moot point. "Working in the field of education is a hard job at this juncture."

One way Administrator 4's district has addressed budget cuts is to go to a four-day week. This has been a common trend among small schools across the country. In Administrator 4's case, his high school aligned their time with the elementary school, but the decision was also driven by sports. The elementary school is in session from 8 a.m.–4 p.m. The prior schedule of 8 a.m.–3 p.m. permitted after school remediation to occur from 3 p.m.–4 p.m.; that time has been lost and the resulting plummet in test scores attest to the fact that the remediation time was valuable. As a solution to this most recent issue, this next school year remediation and enrichment will occur during the school day from 3 p.m.–4 p.m.

Administrator 4 submits that year round school with July off and breaks between each quarter for teachers to recharge would be a positive approach to education. He recalls trying to schedule the week of hunting season off because of the high student absenteeism rate which in turn affects money brought in to the district that is assessed based on attendance. Parents were adamantly opposed to this recommendation even though a plethora of data was presented to delineate the benefit of this idea. He expounds that having the resources to hold summer school positively impacts students' skills and knowledge as indicated by their test scores.

When students attended summer school, their fall test scores were always improved when compared to their spring test scores. Conversely, students who did not attend summer school but should because they were behind always had lower fall test scores when compared to their spring test scores. "It was 100 percent both ways, so we have data that shows skills are lost over the summer. We know this is occurring, but the community is highly resistant to change."

Acquiring appropriate ancillary staff can be challenging. Administrator 5 comments that when hired, ancillary personnel often don't stay. In the past, her speech language pathologist (SLP) was a district employee who also worked for two other districts. The SLP retired and the district could not find anyone to fill the position. To alleviate this issue with students who are speech-language impaired (SLI), she is currently considering transitioning to an online system. She contracts with occupational therapists (OTs) who work with students twice a month. She used to contract for psychological services but will not have to do that this year because one of her teachers is qualified to test students. She currently does not have students with physical therapy (PT) needs.

Administrator 4 interjects that many personnel are shared with other districts. For example their information technology specialist is shared with two other districts and his clerk works for another district part time. This is a result of being a small school and the budget cuts that were made. However, finding OTs, PTs and SLPs prior to the budget cuts was a nightmare because these therapists did not want to travel between districts as their salary did not justify the time that was required to do so. Thus, hiring special educators who are qualified to do testing is a huge help; otherwise, it costs a small fortune to have a specialist come once a month for testing purposes. Another issue is that specialists who do work with the district's students do so for a short time and then leave for private practice because they can make more money.

Administrator 5 adds that when the district had their own SLP, who was a district employee, she observed students in the classrooms and was an active participant in IEP meetings. She continuously told teachers what they could listen for that was related to the speech language goal and how they could respond with corrective action. She sent work home to parents and invited them to sit in on sessions. When the SLP retired, her replacement was a recent graduate who was completely overwhelmed; hence the thoughts about the online system.

Administrator 4 explains that the district has an interactive classroom so the capability to connect with other districts, the State Department or other agencies that also have an interactive classroom exists. He believes this may be the wave of the future, not only with SLI students but for other classes as well. The issue is that some students do well with the online format but others do not. To be successful with online programs one must be self-motivated.

Currently, some students are taking elective classes such as psychology or forensics in the online format. However, the adult in the room is not content certified. Furthermore, only the high-end self-motivated student who likes to learn is thriving in that atmosphere. Moreover, for students in credit recovery or who are preparing for the state standardized test, online programs do not appear to result in successful outcomes. Credit recovery occurs through Administrator 4's state's Digital Learning Academy. Assume a student fails the first semester of sophomore English. Although the student could retake the failed course, he would be reassigned to the same teacher because in a small school only one instructor teaches that course. This has not always been a successful strategy.

A solution has been for the student to retake the course with the Digital Learning Academy online program. The pretest determines what the student has mastered; subsequent instruction only occurs in content that has not been mastered. The upside is students have alternatives to pass a class that was failed; the downside is students have learned they do not have to pass the class with their teacher as they can take this online course. Subsequently, a student might do very little work for their teacher because it is known the online course is available and the failing grade will be replaced with the passing grade earned through this program.

This begs the question how to meet the students' needs in the first place. Discussion revolves around whether or not the class is challenging enough, if the curriculum is too boring, if the student simply tired of sitting by the time a particular class occurs and so forth. "Many of today's students don't care about grades and are often satisfied with producing the minimal work required. Grades are not a motivator like in generations past." Learning is often not a priority; it has been replaced with socialization. Motivating students who are intrinsically unmotivated is a huge challenge.

"There seem to be too many distractions such as electronics, too much free time and too many choices coupled with parents who don't require their child to complete tasks." Administrator 4 recognizes that about 75 percent of his parents are grateful when they are contacted regarding an issue with their child. The other 25 percent tend to blame the teacher for their child's deficits.

Parents claim teachers are asking too much of their child or that there is not enough time for homework completion. Administrator 5 interjects the typical parent response is, "You do whatever *you* need to do."

Many students lack direction regarding what they want to do with their lives. When prompted to have this discussion, they balk as many are satisfied to live at home. Administrator 4 surmises only 10 percent of the students will remain in the area and work on the local ranches as many of the former job opportunities have become mechanized. Approximately 40 percent of the students will leave the area for other work and not return, and approximately 50 percent of the students will go to college. However, only 30 percent of the students who enter college will complete their program of study and obtain a two- or four-year degree. For this reason, they are encouraged to begin at a junior college as the transition would be easier because they come from a small town.

Due to the lack of scholarship funds, many students cannot attend college. Therefore, most students need training in the trade industry such as in a craft or technical program, or they need to attend a junior college. The local economy is unable to support them; there are no job opportunities for them to earn a living wage because there are no major industries or businesses in the area. "Our students would benefit most with degrees in the trades such as welding, diesel mechanics or machinist because other jobs are not in demand."

Students are leaving small communities for places such as the oil fields of North Dakota. Almost all of the students who leave do so because there is no work available; if they stay they will live in poverty. "The middle class in our area has virtually disappeared because the saw mill, Forest Service and timber industry that used to exist has vanished. The only people remaining in our area are older people who have paid off their house."

Similarly, people are not moving into small communities. Hiring teachers has become very difficult because they have no reason to go to all the expense and effort to attain their degree only to be paid a poor wage, have few benefits and be buried with demands. "There is no incentive to become an educator." Administrator 4 comments that his state decided to increase academic requirements, which in essence is the standards. However, this well-intentioned decision did not consider that college students needed encouragement to become teachers to meet the increased academic demand. One way this could be accomplished is by providing incentives such as tuition payback.

The result has been a deficit in math teachers, a problem that was self-created. The education community tried to get their legislators on board by emphasizing the need to align the increased math requirement with increased math teachers. However, this did not happen. The attempt to solve one problem merely created another. "This seems to be an ongoing issue within education, which is probably a result of it being highly political. Everybody, especially the legislature, envisions themselves as an expert in education."

One way Administrator 4's state seems to be addressing the need for teachers is by hiring instructors who have attained alternative certification. Their lack of training means they are the equivalent of student teachers who require a significant amount of training and support. They have passed an entry-level test but they lack practical skills. If a good solid person is willing to be mentored the first year, they can usually survive. However, most people who have taught in Administrator 4's district with an alternative certification do not last.

He speculates that if they had gone through a university degreed program when they attempted to student teach they would have "washed up" or they would have realized that teaching is not where their talent lies. He clarifies his perception by acknowledging that some alternative certification programs such as Teach for America have much stricter guidelines than other programs and can therefore be more successful. He believes, "Some of teaching can be taught, but a lot of it is intrinsic. Educators have to deal with people and without good people skills content knowledge is ineffectual."

INCLUSIVE PRACTICES

When a student is transitioning from the elementary to the high school, the elementary teacher meets with the high school teacher to review all students' IEPs, accommodations, modifications and any other strategies that are effective. Thus, a mini IEP is held to discuss pertinent information for each student. Additionally, the elementary special education teacher discloses the best time in the day to schedule a student's direct instruction that is delineated in their IEP.

Students are educated with their general education peers approximately 90 percent of the time in both the elementary and the high school environment. Administrator 4 comments that, in the high school environment, a student on an IEP will be placed in a resource class to receive specific instruction in the area of disability instead of being placed in a general education elective class. An exception might be a student that has a severe disability who might attend all elective classes and work on functional life skills that will be practical in the post-secondary setting. "Being engaged in hands-on activities is beneficial."

In the elementary environment, to maximize the skills of both the certified and classified faculty, students on IEPs with the same skill level go to the resource room at the same time to receive support. For example, the aide might work with one group, such as the cognitively impaired (CI) students (under the direction of the special education teacher) while the certified teacher works with learning disabled students in reading. Thus, students are rotated into the resource environment throughout the day to work on information from their classroom(s) as needed based on their disability.

The full-time special educator in the high school works with students in a resource environment. They are grouped according to skill level; however, instruction is also individualized. In all cases, instruction is driven by the IEP. To reiterate, students are attending their content classes while receiving their resource support as an elective, so the service being rendered is integrated with the classroom instruction and never disjointed.

Administrator 4 reflects on his experience with special education students in the bigger school district where he first worked versus his current small one. In the larger school, he recalls going into the special education classroom where there was a certified teacher with two aides and 25 students. Many times everyone was working on something not remotely related to what was being taught in the general education core content classes. Teachers were working with too many students at one time to be effective; it was impossible to coordinate instruction with their general education colleagues. He feels fortunate to be working in a small district because, in spite of not having resources or a nice building, general education classes have only 15 to 18 students.

Regarding curricular issues for classrooms with included students, Administrator 5 affirms most teachers have very high standards for their students. She surmises, however, that inclusion tends to have a negative impact on high-performing and gifted students. Some teachers struggle to deal effectively with special education students because they have too many students to teach. They therefore believe their instruction will move forward at a reasonable pace only if they dummy down the curriculum. Thus, many resources are utilized to support the neediest students while the high-performing and gifted students suffer.

Administrator 4 responds that attempts to support students occur in many different ways. For example, there is a reading club at the elementary level with advanced readers. Parents of high-performing students have voiced their concerns regarding their child's needs being met but he does not believe that this concern exists simply because special education students are in the classroom. Administrator 5 affirms that good teachers should be differentiating instruction to meet the needs of all students, particularly the lower level student. However, this should not occur at the expense of those who are high-performing or gifted. Every classroom has a wide variety of levels (usually three) that need instruction within a designated time frame, yet teachers have a limit to what they are able to do in a day.

One strategy to support the needs of all students in the classroom is peer tutoring. Every student that is new to either the elementary or the high school is assigned to a peer for the purpose of learning how to navigate different areas of the school or how to meet a teacher's expectations. Academic peer tutoring needs are determined as the school year progresses occur in an informal manner on a case-by-case basis. For example, students who mesh may be teamed up or seniors might tutor students in their math class. A general education student never knows that the person he is tutoring might be someone with a disability. Peer tutoring can be a student's senior project. "When peer tutoring is used, it has been very effective."

SENIOR REQUIREMENTS

Every senior must write a research paper, perform a community service activity and complete an individual project. Students must complete forms, obtain a mentor, describe the resources needed and execute an oral presentation in front of a committee that satisfactorily meets the requirements delineated on a rubric. The project is the students' choice, something that they would like to do within their area of interest. Examples include working with somebody in the community building an engine, completing an art project with students in the elementary school or writing a book. The end goal is to create a product or demonstrate what was learned.

"We believe this is one of the best things we do and we would like to expand this program. It is student-driven; the students really get into their projects because they have the ability to make choices. It's a great motivator; kids are in charge of their own learning often choosing projects that are hands-on." The success of many projects is the result of having a good motivated teacher mentor.

TECHNOLOGY

In Administrator 4's district, all of the buildings are wired for high-speed Internet. Each classroom has three or four computers, there is a complete computer lab with twenty-five computers at the elementary school and there are two complete labs with twenty-five computers at the high school. Furthermore, there are computers in the resource room for student use with books on tape and the Dragon Naturally Speaking program that transcribes spoken words. The elementary school has a software program called Programmed Logic for Automatic Teaching Operations (PLATO). Moreover, the high school uses PLATO to provide opportunities for credit recovery, extended learning and alternative routes to graduation.

PLATO engages students with interactive media-rich content that is standards-based, aligned to Common Core State Standards and grounded in sound pedagogy. Covering a wide range of core subjects and electives, the software can be used with students at any level—those who have learning deficits, those who are at grade level, and those who are advanced. Teachers can opt to use PLATO as their main classroom instruction or as a supplement to their classroom instruction. Students can test out of the content they have already mastered, allowing them to concentrate on concepts with which they struggle. Assessments are integrated with each course to ensure students demonstrate proficiency before moving to the next concept.

The elementary school has also utilized a program called Study Island for the past two years. Study Island is a web-based program customized to help students meet the standards in their state. A supplemental tool, the mini-lessons provide instant feedback. For example, correct answers result in a yellow star appearing; wrong answers result in detailed explanations and prompts that assist the student. Study Island is adaptable (the teacher can select specific content and the number of questions to be completed) and goal oriented (the teacher can select the percent correct that constitutes mastery).

It also provides remediation (incorrect answers result in a student being cycled down to a lower level until they demonstrate mastery at the more basic level). Regretfully, Study Island will not be used in the upcoming year due to budget cuts. "Study Island was beneficial because it was very interactive." Administrator 4 asserts that having a person available to provide instruction is usually preferable over technology, but it is nice to have both. "Losing the ability to have some good software like Study Island is detrimental to students."

DATA

Administrators 4 and 5 do not have any data to determine if inclusion is preferable to pull-out resource instruction because the district is small and all of their students are included in their content classes. However, Administrator 5 states that in her prior district no student on an IEP was ever exited from special education services. Conversely, students who enter her current district in the second grade are typically exited in the sixth or seventh grade unless they are severely disabled. Administrator 4 laments that there is not enough time or resources to work with and exit students when they enter the district in the later grades. "Often there is not enough time to satisfactorily remediate and help a student who comes to us late, for example in the 10th grade. We need to get them younger when we can have adequate time to get them to grade level."

Clearly, any student who enters the district and stays for a sufficient amount of time to receive services has their issues sufficiently addressed to the point they can be exited. Both administrators take great pride in their ability to help students to this extent. Administrator 4 emphasizes this is made possible because of good teaching and having good personnel. "It's not technology, textbooks or resources. We may be a financially poor district and lack the parent support that we desire, but I let my staff know that we have small student to teacher ratios and there is no excuse to not move students forward."

Administrator 5 gathers academic data in the elementary school as benchmarks in the fall, winter and spring in the areas of reading, math concepts and math applications using the AimsWeb program. AimsWeb is a web-based data management and reporting system. Designed to screen and monitor progress, AimsWeb uses short, valid and reliable general outcome measures for K–8 reading and math aptitudes that can be appropriately integrated with any curriculum. AimsWeb assessment probes meet professional standards and provide a standardized testing platform. In Administrator 5's school, the data is used to place incoming students, decide who needs Title I services and to determine academic growth.

State data that breaks information into smaller subgroups is also distributed to teachers. Administrator 4 is able to track students rather intimately because his high school is so small. He has found students' daily performance to be more reflective of their ability than results from a standardized test such as the state exam. School data permits teachers to consult with their colleagues and consistently guide students by considering their grades and attendance. If a student is falling behind, the issue is noted quickly and stopgap measures are implemented immediately. "Students are not able to anonymously shut down by fading into the woodwork, and this is not just the special education student."

STANDARDS

Administrator 4 continues by describing his concern about the Common Core State Standards (CCSS). "We are under no illusion about the Common Core Standards. We are expecting a pretty good push back from both parents and students." Most of the staff understands that students need a rigorous program. Most of the students have learned the standardized system required by NCLB. Upping the stakes to more critical thinking is going to be challenging but change is not a bad thing. CCSS will force teachers to refocus and reconsider what they are doing in the classroom. Classroom instruction will have to be reinvented, which is going to require a bit of thought. Administrator 4 is also a teacher, so he is well aware of his staff concerns.

All teachers at the secondary level have already been informed that they will be doing Common Core assessments aligned to the type of questions found on the new Smarter Balanced Assessment (SBA). They will have to show that content of their assessments in their courses, such as for their end-of-course assessments such as final exams, are asking higher level questions.

Those who teach electives will also be required to integrate technical reading and writing because everyone is responsible for improving student growth. "Improvement is a school-wide goal."

Administrator 4 believes NCLB was a detour that required a great deal of resources for low-end students but which ignored the gifted and talented students. Focusing on struggling students is a good thing, but getting *all* students to think so they can function in the world by analyzing their environment and problem solving is imperative. He does not believe his curriculum will need to be supplanted because CCSS is much more process oriented. It involves how one teaches, what their assessments look like and evaluates how students are processing the material as opposed to just asking content questions and scoring answers as right or wrong. The goal of CCSS is to change the way students evaluate a problem, which is a very transferable skill. Remembering specific problems from a class is not what's important; rather, developing processing and higher order thinking skills is what's important.

Administrator 5 agrees that current texts will be a guide. Standards drive *what* is being taught but not *how* it is being taught. The focus will be on teaching students how to analyze multiple-step problems without multiple-choice options. Students will need to think, problem solve and collaborate with their peers. She projects the difficulty for teachers is going to be determining how to reconstruct current lessons that encourages students to respond by demonstrating the ability to adeptly think through a question.

Dovetailing off this comment, Administrator 4 comments this is going to be hard for teachers. For example, his government class has a great deal of difficult vocabulary. The curriculum is not changing, so mastering methods to raise the standards by asking appropriate questions while teaching the vocabulary words is going to be a challenge. "Changing the teaching approach to more effectively work with the same curriculum is the challenge."

COLLABORATION WHILE LEADING

Both administrators agree one of their advantages as a small school is having the ability to frequently interact with their teachers. Teachers know their office hours but also have the opportunity to ask questions and get clarification when they see their administrator in the hallway, during lunch or before and after school. Administrator 4 states he can stick his head into a classroom and know immediately whether a teacher is prepared and if good teaching is occurring. Administrator 5 states her teachers work hard and they work together; teachers help teachers, she helps teachers, and teachers help her, "So everyone has a pretty good relationship with each other."

Administrator 4 is pulled in two directions based on the hats he wears as a principal and as a superintendent. As a superintendent, his primary goal is to take care of the board and make sure the schools and the whole district runs well. As a principal, his primary goal is to take care of his building and teachers. Sometimes these goals conflict, especially during negotiations. His teachers expect him to support them and whatever choice they make, but he also has an obligation to the board. Decisions need to be fiscally sound—classified people need to be supported, buses need to run and other issues outside the realm of the classroom need to be appropriately addressed in a timely manner.

Leaders who serve as both superintendents and principals sometimes have loyalties that are at odds with one another. Consequently, the staff may sometimes feel unsupported because they are not provided with every re-source they want. However, approving a pay raise often means resources cannot be attained. Conversely, approving the purchase of resources may mean teachers don't get a pay raise. "This is difficult and very exhausting as an administrator."

To get the school year off to a good start, Administrator 5's elementary staff holds fifteen-minute conferences with every parent the first week of school after teachers return from summer break but prior to the students returning. At that time, teachers review their classroom expectations and explain the school's policies. They also describe how contacts will be made throughout the school year. Administrator 5 describes this process as invalu-able.

Administrator 4 begins the school year by holding a district meeting with board members, bus drivers, classified staff and teachers—every employee is present. He gives a forty-five minute presentation describing the upcoming school year with the purpose of being positive and excited. District goals are shared but the main impetus is emphasizing what positive programs and outcomes are going to occur (versus discussing the lack of funding or sup-plies). Furthermore, the district provides lunch so colleagues within the school community can break bread together.

TRANSITIONING STUDENTS

Transitioning students into their post-secondary environment occurs via many meetings to determine what the child wants to do. Assistance is sought for occupational and job shadowing opportunities. Trips are made to the city at least a couple of times during students' time in high school so that they can job shadow somebody for a couple of days to determine what they like to do. Many students have "aha" moments such as when they realize how they must dress in a business environment. "We try to give them as many of those 'aha' moments as possible."

Administrator 4 expounds that students who live in the city are exposed to different businesses and occupations as they ride by on the bus. Students enrolled in rural small schools do not have the same exposure. Consequently, when they are asked what they want to do after high school they don't really have an idea of the options that are available to them. "In fact, some students do not venture more than fifty miles from our small town." Therefore, their trip to the city with school personnel is their first exposure to something outside of their farming or ranching community. "We are well aware of what our students are missing in this regard."

Discussing transition goals is described as an interesting process. Asking students what their interests are does not mean they have knowledge of the possibilities available to them. Special education students tend to believe they have fewer choices available than their non-disabled peers. They therefore look at themselves as not being as prepared and as lacking the skills that their peers possess. "We try to mitigate this mindset and encourage them to maximize their potential. This is forefront for all of us, but especially our counselor who organizes all the calls, makes all the arrangements, and assists every student with their scholarship applications."

SYSTEMIC IMPROVEMENT

Administrator 4 believes levels should exist, enabling teachers to work with students who are performing at the same level as opposed to an archaic system of scheduling students based on their age. For instance, currently every twelve-year-old is in the same grade regardless of their ability. A leveling system was discussed with the community but they were not amenable to the idea. Admittedly, one of the issues is not having enough aides to support a leveling program.

A solution is to take fourth, fifth and sixth graders and work with specialists—someone teaches math, someone teaches science, and someone teaches language arts at those three grade levels. Students would navigate to the teacher at certain times during the day. This is as close as Administrator 4 has been able to get to effect a leveling system.

Administrator 4 expounds with ideas of reinventing the school system. He would create a year-round calendar and would modify the curriculum with levels through which students could move as quickly as they could. This would enable some sixth-graders to take algebra, which would set them up for calculus by the time they are in high school. Currently, the capability of having students ready for advanced higher order thinking courses is almost nonexistent in his small school. He speculates that big districts have more opportunities to appropriately place students at their skill level.

Administrator 5 voices frustration that pots of money cannot be combined for local schools to do what is best for their students. She dreams of receiving a block grant with the freedom to place challenged students with teachers with whom they have a rapport. She wishes funding and grants were more integrated and administrators were trusted to take the money and use it where it's needed, doing what is best for students. For example, there is no money for an additional special educator who could go into the classroom and support included students. Thus, the current special educator is only able to pull students from their classroom to work with them, "And what does that do to these kids? They feel like, 'I have to go to the dumb table.'" This arrangement prevents the special educator from working with a heterogeneous group of students who can scaffold off of each other's input.

The apparent problem is that lawmakers want accountability for the money districts receive, but they hamstring administrators by permitting funds to be applied only to certain programs. All school districts vary from each other and their needs fluctuate at different times. Students' needs should be driving monetary decisions; money should be used in a way that most effectively meets students' needs at a particular place and time. The lack of flexibility forces administrators to creatively manipulate their funds in order to accomplish their mission. Small schools must be especially creative because they live on grants. "Necessity becomes the mother of invention. There are many large schools that do not use their money nearly as effectively as some of our smaller thriftier schools."

Administrator 5 concludes by saying educating students, parents and educators are vital to success. Students should be educated regarding what their choices are and the resources that are available to them, and parents should be educated regarding what teachers or agencies can provide that will help their child. Teachers should be educated regarding the reality of following the IEP, understanding what can realistically be done for students and accept that all children are different. Students require alternative academic and socio-emotional accommodations based on their internal needs and external environment. Thus, educating everybody needs to be paramount, which requires time and outside resources.

Administrator 4 stresses that educators live in a challenging environment and it takes special people to enter the field. He worries about alternative certification programs that open up the doors to anybody who thinks they can teach but who lack the proper instruction and pedagogy. He also worries that universities are not preparing students appropriately. Additionally teachers are not compensated as well as they should be; educating any population cannot be done "on the cheap." Resources are needed.

He expounds that getting good people to enter the field of education requires a living wage with appropriate benefits. He is concerned that current educators are retiring early while young people are choosing to leave the profession prematurely. Additionally, special educators are extremely overwhelmed with paperwork. The pressure they feel due to the need to work with large numbers of students is driving them out of the profession. Only the most dedicated educators are entering the special education field

He also feels that legislators need to understand that getting the best people into the education profession means money for scholarships needs to be available. Potential teachers need to be identified early, trained properly and be rewarded for entering the profession. This is particularly true for special educators, math and English teachers "because way too much is being asked of them." He believes that people who have a passion for English and teaching it are shocked to learn 60 percent of the reading that is required under the new CCSS is technical versus being focused on literature.

If the system is going to be sustainable, it needs to be revamped. More students than ever before are being identified as special needs; instead of cutting Title I and discretionary funds leaders need to prepare for this situation. Properly dividing thin resources is impossible. The loss of educational funding has resulted in an increase in competing interests, which in turn is driving administrators and teachers out of the profession. The daily grind is becoming too hard.

ROCKY MOUNTAIN REGION TALKING POINTS

Procedures

- Schedule every parent for a fifteen minute teacher conference the first week of school for a review of classroom expectations and school policies.
- Start every school year with an optimistic forty-five minute presentation that describes the positive programs and outcomes that are going to occur.
- Attend educational law seminars that review mandates.
- Turn observed substandard parent/faculty interactions into teachable moments.
- Create a structure that permits frequent general and special educators with opportunities to co-plan.
- Consider the students' needs when creating schedules that honor their LRE.
- Expect personnel new to the field of education to require an abundance of support.
- Offer continuous training regarding differentiated instruction, strategies for layering the curriculum and behavior intervention strategies.

- Provide all new teachers with a mentor in their grade or subject area their first year in the district.
- Present IEP training at the beginning of every school year.
- Extract the accommodations page for teachers to place in their plan books and files for substitute teachers.
- Ensure substitute teachers know where to find their file that contains important information about the students with whom they'll be working.
- Stress accommodations are legal requirements, not options.
- In the spring have teachers who are currently working with a student on an IEP meet with receiving teachers to discuss specific strategies that do and do not work for the student.
- Revisit the above strategies in the fall before the school year begins.

Challenges and Solutions

- Underscore that failure to follow an IEP puts the teacher and district personnel at risk for a lawsuit.
- Emphasize that perfection is not expected but effort is.
- Consider transitioning to a four-day week if budget cuts are severe.
- Provide remediation and enrichment during the last hour of every school day.
- Implement a year-round school calendar to mitigate lost student knowledge during long breaks and to incorporate common local disruptions.
- Implement summer school programs to remediate students' learning gaps and prevent skill and knowledge loss.
- Acquire SLPs via an online system such as Skype if your community is rural or you are otherwise unable to incentivize potential SLP employees.
- Incentivize potential employees through tuition payback programs.
- Consider hiring alternative certified teachers who have completed reputable programs such as Teach for America.
- Offer online classes for motivated self-learners to obtain credit.
- Deliver online courses for credit recovery or state standardized test preparation thoughtfully as only motivated students tend to have successful outcomes.
- Ensure students have opportunities to receive training in the trade industry.

Inclusive Practices

- Ensure teachers of transitioning students hold mini-IEPs to discuss pertinent strategies with receiving teachers.

- Schedule all students into general education content classes and rotate those with the same skill level into resource rooms for support at the same time.
- Use the resource room as a means to support what students are learning in their general education classes, not as a separate entity unto itself.
- Create a reading club and stock library and classroom shelves with advanced reading material to meet the needs of gifted and high-performing students.
- Implement peer tutoring teams on a case-by-case basis.
- Require every senior to write a research paper, perform a community service activity and complete an individual project of their choice.

Technology

- Install the most up-to-date technology possible.
- Purchase student software that is interactive, promotes creativity and provides instant feedback.

Data

- Gather and distribute academic data in the fall, winter and spring that divide information into useable subgroups.
- Utilize data to correctly program incoming students.
- Use data to consistently guide decisions by implementing stop-gap measures.

Standards

- Obtain resources that help students develop critical thinking skills.
- Provide training regarding technical reading and writing skills.
- Teach students to process situations, not just regurgitate information.
- Help teachers determine how to reconstruct approaches to current lessons so students are encouraged to respond after adeptly thinking through a question.

Supporting All Transitioning Students

- Provide a means for teachers to effect occupational and job shadowing opportunities.

Systemic Improvement

- Consider leveling students, enabling teachers to work with students who are at the same stage of learning.
- Provide opportunities for students to move through levels at their own pace.
- Permit local schools to determine how to best use money allotted to them (with an accountability system in place).
- Educate students regarding choices and resources available to them.
- Educate parents regarding what teachers or agencies can provide that will help their child.
- Identify potential teachers early, provide rigorous training and allot scholarship money as an incentive.
- Maintain Title I and discretionary funds to sustain the cost of educating exceptional students.

Chapter Five

Administrator 6: Southeast Region

Administrator 6 began his fourteen-year education career in the southeast region as a high school social studies teacher. After two-and-a-half years he transitioned to a middle school where he taught mathematics for two years. He attended graduate school and then interned at the middle school level. Subsequently, he became an assistant principal at two different high schools and at an elementary school. For the past four years he has been the principal at the middle school where he interned for his principal certificate.

Approximately 650 students attend Administrator 6's middle school and approximately 11 percent of those are exceptional. Although his school ranks in the bottom 25th percentile of his state, his composite score continues to increase. His students are not meeting or exceeding standards (they have only met AYP once in the past ten years) but their proficiency is improving. Administrator 6 believes the reason more improvement has not occurred is that the needs of the exceptional student population are not being properly addressed. Also, many average and high-performing students are not having their needs met. Consequently, there has not been a concerted effort to ensure that each group is getting the additional resources needed to be successful.

Administrator 6 affirms a reorganization of the resources that were already in existence when he became principal could help. Because his school does not receive Title I funds, money that helps schools similar to his are not available. He therefore has to be very creative obtaining funds, putting social programs together, focusing on leadership and motivating students. He emphasizes the importance of motivating students, teachers and parents, which takes a multi-pronged approach. He is proud that his efforts resulted in exceptional students being integrated into general education classrooms.

"They are no longer the kids that nobody else wants. They are actually performing above their general education peers as far as their growth." Administrator 6 focuses heavily on growth because the number of low-performing students entering his school has increased every year. "When you have students entering a middle school who do not know the alphabet or who cannot read on the first grade level, they are not going to magically be able to pass a test at the eighth grade level." He therefore focuses on growth for these vulnerable students, especially those with exceptionalities. Subsequently, his students "exceeded growth" for three consecutive years in reading. The data is not available for the 2012–2013 school year due to his district transitioning to the Common Core State Standards (CCSS).

IDENTIFYING EXCEPTIONAL STUDENTS

Administrator 6 does not believe all of his current exceptional students should be qualified to receive exceptional program services as some of those identified are economically disadvantaged, not disabled. These students are often academically far behind their peers because their former teachers lacked sufficient resources to address their deficiencies when they were at the elementary level. Subsequently, impoverished students sometimes enter his school with substantial gaps in their learning, not with a disability. However, because teachers want extra help for their students, they perceive that placing them in exceptional programs is the only way to obtain the requisite support.

This has been an issue over several years. "Many students could have been average to high performers if they had initially had access to the right resources." Also, some students who are a bit antsy or rambunctious are inappropriately referred by teachers who do not want to put up with their mischief. For those who are appropriately placed in the smaller setting, Administrator 6 believes that, "Sometimes the smaller setting is good for students, but sometimes it is not. If the right teacher and assistant are not in the room, the placement is a disaster for both the teacher and the students."

Moreover, some parents attempt to have their child identified for services, not realizing they are doing their child a disservice in the long run. Unlike most districts in which parents insist their child needs services as a means of circumnavigating arduous academic requirements, parents in Administrator 6's school request services thinking the smaller setting means their child will receive a more rigorous curriculum. "They want accommodations because they think they are giving their child an extra edge." A couple of years ago, a parent wanted to circumnavigate the response to intervention process. The attention deficit hyperactive disordered (ADHD) student was on a 504 plan and was making As and Bs. In three years he was never a problem, but the parent fought for him to receive accommodations mistakenly believing a placement in exceptional programs meant academic supports existed that were superior to what was received in the general education environment.

INCLUSION PHILOSOPHY AND BUY-IN STRATEGIES

Administrator 6 always believed more students should be included instead of excluded. Over the years, he has understood that a teacher's lack of training can cause hesitancy to include exceptional students in general education classrooms. "A substantial amount of training is required to become certified to teach in a regular education classroom. When including exceptional students with behavioral and learning difficulties is discussed without resources or training to manage the classroom or differentiate instruction, I can see the reluctance."

When he became principal at his middle school, Administrator 6 recognized his special educators were overwhelmed. They were expected to work with limited resources and no instructional aides (IAs) with multiple needy students requiring various layers of assistance. He therefore suggested that his teachers collaborate, receive some training and co-teach, teaming strong general and special educators. "Two highly qualified people can handle a diverse population with better results than casting students into a corner in a room that is chaotic."

One strategy Administrator 6 used to gain faculty buy-in into the inclusion concept was to discuss baseline data that clearly showed his teachers where their students were performing. He asked them if they wanted their school and students to be successful or if they were okay with having "throw-away kids." He asked them if they were teachers for all students or just for those who were easiest to work with because they don't cause any trouble. He inquired if their own child had a disability, would they be satisfied to have them placed in a room all day with one teacher who is overworked and overwhelmed.

CO-TEACHING

The result was his highest performing teachers volunteered to co-teach. For instance, one special educator, who had phenomenal results when she worked alone, volunteered to co-teach with an outstanding general education colleague. From that point forward, all students with learning disabilities were scheduled to participate with their general education peers 100 percent of the time. A targeted reading program was taught in a ninety-minute block. Low functioning exceptional students in math, reading or both were programmed into a classroom with ten low performing students who did not have a disability.

Students were co-taught with targeted interventions for the first half of the period and supplemented with regular standard course of study for the second half of the period. Benchmarks for implementing inclusion did not have to be created, "they just happened as the teachers moved forward." Administrator 6 periodically asked his teachers what they needed and discussed what was going well and what was not working; the program was tweaked accordingly. Academic benchmarks existed in the math and targeted reading program via the Vmath and Vreader software program.

Vmath delivers modular-based instruction that is a results-driven and research-based intervention. It is an effective tool for Tier II students who require targeted math support that complements their core instruction. Provided in thirty to forty-five minute increments, students work on vital foundational math concepts and develop higher-order thinking problem-solving strategies. The web-based *VmathLive* environment enables students to improve skills at their own pace, often exceeding more than one year of math knowledge in a year's timeframe.

Similarly, Vreader is an interactive e-reading system that enables students to learn pre-reading skills and then acquire words that help them read fluently. Students also practice reading comprehension, vocabulary, phonics, word-building and definitions. The stories are animated with voice, graphics and music. Words are highlighted as Vreader speaks them. If the student touches an unknown word on the screen, the Vreader pronounces it for them. There is also a list of vocabulary words at the beginning of each story that, when touched, Vreader shows the definition and verbally reads it. Some of the words have follow-up questions to ensure the student understands the definition of the word.

Administrator 6 emphasizes that establishing a co-teaching environment is a process, but insists that a leader does not acknowledge what is a best practice only to ignore the strategy. With the proper training and supports in place, teachers are less resistant and learn how to fully manage the program, leaving no one to deal with failure. He built his faculty up and appealed to their emotional side by saying, "Imagine this is your child, would you want him or her to have access to these programs? They did not ask to be born with their deficiencies, so what are we going to do to help them?"

Teachers volunteered to be teamed up the first year inclusion was implemented. Administrator 6 stated what needed to get done and asked who was willing to step up and do what it took. Enough personnel volunteered that teams were easily formed. Furthermore, the teams got along well prior to this as colleagues, so no work had to be done to match personalities.

Additionally, the director of exceptional programs presented videos regarding how co-teaching should look and his teachers immediately grasped the general premise. He did not provide follow-up training mainly because he had "a phenomenal group of teachers that just wanted to make things happen so this took on a life of its own. They worked together for the children." They also knew their administrator's expectations and were able to work with minimal supervision.

The next year, the local university provided a grant to promote inclusion and universal design, a process in which teachers consider the environment and other conditions when adapting instruction. Thus, teachers were incentivized to implement inclusion via their perks of SMART Boards, a set of computers and a SMART interactive response system. The SMART system facilitates the learning process by permitting teachers to instantly assess both formative and summative learning, thereby increasing student participation and improving learning outcomes. All teachers who volunteered to work with exceptional students or co-teach received SMART Boards and additional technology because they volunteered to assist the most vulnerable children.

"Although that was one way I promoted inclusion, without these incentives teachers stepped [up] and said, 'We will be more than happy to do this.'" His teachers' willingness to be proactive mitigated the usual difficulties administrators face when transitioning to a different schoolwide structure. "I was blessed, my teachers just wanted to make this happen."

Additionally, these were some of Administrator 6's stronger teachers who worked well with parents and students. The co-teaching environment permitted teachers to learn about each other's population and which strategies were appropriate, resulting in positive outcomes that are not easily attainable when working in a segregated environment all day. Co-teachers reached out to their special education colleagues, which helped them gain skills and become better educators. When inclusion was implemented, general educators who were not in co-teaching teams rarely had exceptional students scheduled into their classrooms. The exception was high functioning students who could succeed in courses such as pre-algebra. Decisions were made on a case-by-case basis.

There were two co-teaching teams in each grade. One team taught math, the other team taught reading. Students were fully included in social studies and science without a special educator in the room. Administrator 6 attempted to have no more than two-thirds of the students in a classroom with exceptionalities, but that was sometimes difficult. For example, one school year opened with eighteen sixth-graders identified as exceptional; by the end of the first week, twelve more exceptional students had enrolled or were identified from summer testing for a total of thirty.

The above situation forced Administrator 6 to reorganize and place all of the exceptional students with one co-teaching team for their math and reading classes. His highest growth math and reading teachers volunteered to co-teach these students, determined to give them the best instruction available. This required a complete revamping of their schedule. "They did a phenomenal job. I never had any discipline issues with this class; students were learning."

Among the above students, six were placed in a self-contained class because they were so low. One girl had already been retained twice in elementary school, barely knew the alphabet and did not know how to write her
name. Another student was similar to her; neither was being successful in the
inclusion setting, so a more appropriate environment for those two students
was created. Eventually, four other severely academically low students were
added. The result was that the remaining twenty-four included students were
successfully progressing. "I hated to do this, but it became a legal issue. The
parent was upset and constantly proclaiming her child could not do the work
in the general education environment."

Administrator 6 eventually challenged the parent and said, "I keep hearing you say what she can't do, but what can she do? I want to place her where
she will be able to do something when she leaves this middle school. At some
point, she needs to learn how to be productive; otherwise she will need
someone to take care of her the rest of her life." The parent understood what
was being said and the importance of the message.

"Accepting the reality of an exceptionality is difficult but important.
Working together so students are productive and feel a sense of accomplishment is paramount. Throwing children into a room and not including them as
part of the school is counterintuitive." In this case, the child was "good at
helping others." Thus, when at the elementary level, teachers permitted her to
leave her classroom to go to a lower grade and "help" younger students.
Consequently, she did not receive her own instruction resulting in not knowing how to write her name. It was a disservice to her for teachers to keep her
happy by letting her do what she wanted instead of teaching her.

Keeping students happy is not preparing them for reality. Administrator 6
told another parent that life does not consist of separate settings. "We have
got to learn how to get along with people. Your child cannot hit others
because she is frustrated when she cannot do her work. The time for excuses
is over. Your child will not learn overnight, but we have got to start some-
where." Although not initially happy, the parent understood. Teachers and
parents knew Administrator 6's expectations and delivered.

PERSONNEL

Administrator 6 always believed in inclusion, but getting the appropriate
structure in place requires an appropriate budget. He remarks that if he had
been able to hire one more teacher, "I could have done so much more." One
more IA or certified teacher would have been very helpful. Lacking personnel constrains what can be done with a program.

Administrator 6 has not experienced entrenchment of general educators
engaging in an "us" vs. "them" stance. Some of the younger teachers have

been more willing to work with exceptional students than other younger teachers. Similarly some of the more experienced teachers were more apprehensive than their colleagues to work with exceptional students. However, they know they are going to work with exceptional students on a rotating basis because it is not fair to put exceptional students with the same teachers all of the time. The inclusion program initially started with volunteers; however, teachers know they are expected to take their turn.

Administrator 6 liked to place his IAs in the general education classroom. He found it interesting that after he opted to implement the inclusion model, the district cut his IA from his school stating she was no longer needed. He therefore had a valuable resource taken away because he implemented a best practice and moved away from segregated self-contained resource classrooms. "It is counterproductive to agree that inclusion is the best program to implement only to take away a resource that could make the program better."

When he did have an IA, she floated to different classrooms where the greatest academic or behavioral need existed. She was "top notch" with strong abilities to work with exceptional students. In fact, she was so good that Administrator 6 would tease her and jokingly ask her what position she wanted to work in the following year. She ultimately became a behavior coach because she was good with the students, did her job well and was very well prepared.

Administrator 6 does not have any hard data to demonstrate that students perform better both academically as well as behaviorally in an inclusive environment. This is because his exceptional students are on a modified testing module and their scores are not reported in the same way as their general education peers. However, behavior incidents have decreased and end of grade data show an upward trend for all students. Moreover, based on feeder high school anecdotal data and lowered dropout and discipline rates, "It is clear our eighth grade students are better prepared as they transition to the high school environment."

SHARING A VISION

To convey his vision to his faculty members, Administrator 6 begins the year by doing a presentation about yearly goals and what was accomplished the prior year. Inclusion and co-teaching is included in the presentation. Throughout the year, he readdresses different aspects of his vision during faculty meetings. Team leaders meet with him individually and then convey information discussed to their team members. He avoids asking teachers to read articles that describe positive strategies because he recognizes their time is limited. However, if he finds something of extreme interest, he sends an email highlighting the important aspect of what he read or the link to the article.

Administrator 6 did not receive instruction regarding how to develop inclusive programs. He credits his mother, a pre-kindergarten teacher, for developing his ability to be a forward thinker. Also, as the sibling of an exceptional brother, he understood at an early age the importance of treating people with respect. "I always felt we should treat people the way we want to be treated." He does not place students in one chaotic room all day without anyone checking to see their progress is the correct approach.

"I have always been a service-oriented person who does whatever it takes to get the job done. I understand in many instances we educators are the parents to our students. We therefore need to step up to the plate and do whatever needs to be done to treat our students as if they were our own children—even the ones who are more challenging." The more congenial students who follow directions and stay on task are going to be fine; not that they don't also deserve rigorous instruction, but it's the students who are struggling to find their way that really need more intense attention and instruction. "Otherwise, we are setting up our students for failure."

Administrator 6 recalls taking a business class in which he read a pamphlet titled, "The Only Game in Town" that talked about how public schools have to compete with charter and private schools. He knew then he wanted students and parents to choose his school because "we develop winners." He knew he had to put programs in place that would attract students and enable them to access the same opportunities as their richer neighbors. Raised in a city with a diverse population, he values the knowledge that everyone brings to the table.

The most important thing Administrator 6 has at his disposal to fulfill his vision of inclusion is his top-notch teachers. They have the mindset that inclusion is important and they are going to make it happen. Ideally, he could use more personnel, but most importantly, teachers must have the mindset that they are educators for all students, not just a few. "People who enter the field of education must have a good heart. You can't train a bad heart. Educators have to care about all children."

STANDARDIZED TESTS

Administrator 6 believes standardized testing can be overdone but that assessing what is being taught to determine if any learning is occurring is essential. Testing is not necessarily bad, but testing intellectually disabled students, especially those who are nonverbal due to the severity of their condition, seems inappropriate. Otherwise, data that informs educators as to whether or not their students are learning is valuable. Administrator 6 notes with pride that some of his exceptional students out-performed his general education students. He deduces that success is not just a product of the skill set a student has when he enters the classroom but what is done for the child when present. He asserts that administrators need to determine how successful teachers are moving their students in a positive direction so their strategies can be emulated.

As far as the Common Core State Standards, Administrator 6 finds being presented with so much information at one time to be a bit daunting. However, he believes in four or five years educators will appreciate that the bold step of implementing CCSS was made. He believes the requirements are what teachers should be doing and what students should be learning. He further believes educators brought CCSS on themselves by being full of excuses as to why certain students can't achieve, why certain students drop out of school and why students lack basic knowledge when they are ready to graduate. "Millions of dollars and a plethora of resources have been distributed among the states Therefore, comments that CCSS is unrealistic, has been imposed upon educators or that we don't have the resources (as was the case with No Child Left Behind) is not acceptable."

Administrator 6 asserts that hearing new complaints that CCSS expectations are now too copious comes from educators who will never be happy. "We need to quit with the excuses." Administrator 6 expounds, "While I lack the ability to be a rocket scientist, it should not be assumed that I am incapable of learning and should therefore be relegated to dig ditches the rest of my life. Similarly, to think we don't have to teach or expose students to concepts is unacceptable."

As a participating state in the Race to the Top (RTT) program, Administrator 6 muses that the very people who said they don't have the money and resources to be successful now have an opportunity to earn these funds, but they are complaining. He believes RTT is a well-intended program and he speculates that five years from now communities will appreciate the work that has been put into its implementation. He asserts that the standards that exist have been in place for years, they just didn't have a name. The assessments will continue to evolve and will get better with time. "Teachers will learn to teach information that is assessed and students will learn the information."

TEACHER EVALUATIONS

Teachers are now being evaluated via their growth component, which is based on student outcomes. Most teachers are accepting of this new system. "Judging teachers based on student proficiency would be a problem. However, judging a teacher on how much growth their students incurred from the day they enter the classroom to the day they are tested is a different matter. It establishes how effective a teacher is with individual students as opposed to blaming a teacher when a student does not pass a test. Measuring the skill of a teacher via student growth is appropriate."

PARENT COMMUNICATION

Administrator 6 asserts the most effective way his parents become informed of current or upcoming events is via his phone-calling system that automatically sends messages to them. He can record his announcements and the automatic dial system transmits them immediately. The benefit is parents are receiving timely phone calls for reasons other than what their child has done wrong; that is, they receive positive messages. He also has "Wednesday Folders." Parents know to inspect their child's folders every Wednesday for information. Furthermore, some of his teachers have developed their own web page, but most of them communicate information via email.

THE DEFINING MOMENT

Administrator 6 describes his defining moment as something that occurred his first year as an administrator. There were a number of students who had moved on to the high school that were constantly in the newspaper "for having done bad things." He asked his teachers if they ever got tired of seeing their former students in the news or hearing about students who had dropped out of school. He emphasized that those are "our" kids. After working with them, they transition to the high school and then drop out. Teachers responded, "Yes, we are tired of hearing the bad news," instead of "Oh well, it's not our fault."

He followed that question by asking his faculty what they believed they could do differently to better prepare these children. Everyone was very engaged and participated in a lengthy discussion regarding solutions that were different, bold and new. The result was adopting a leadership program called "The 7 Habits of Highly Effective Teens." Wanting to develop his students into leaders and ensure everyone, including the teachers, fully understood the seven habits, Administrator 6 brought in a local consultant who provided training for all.

In brief, via the seven habits, students and faculty learned to be proactive (understand they are responsible for creating their own happiness); begin with the end in mind (develop a personal mission statement to guide the decision-making process); put first things first (learn to prioritize); think win-win (celebrate others' success); seek first to understand then to be understood (develop active listening skills); synergy (work together to create a better product than what could be created alone); and how to self-renew (strengthening one's body, heart, brain and soul). His staff understood that everyone needed to work together because there is a real world beyond the walls of the middle school in which their students will need to function.

Remarkably, the teachers' initial concern for keeping their at-risk students in school prompted future discussions such as how to improve the performance of exceptional and higher performing students. For example, the higher functioning students were not meeting academic standards every year; they were lazy and just passing because they were smart. Ensuring they were meeting their potential was a challenge.

Importantly, Administrator 6 permitted his teachers to drive the discussion and determine what needed to be done. "I always believed in gaining buy-in and not leading from the top down. Building a program should occur from the bottom up." When he learned that the positive behavior support matrix (that was in place when he took over as principal) was something that teachers believed was being imposed upon them, he permitted them to redevelop it.

Thus, he again obtained buy-in using his bottom up approach. "Things snowballed from there. We moved slowly; change did not happen overnight." The slow but steady bottom up approach empowered teachers and accomplished the task of developing better strategies that were easily understood.

ADDRESSING CHALLENGING STUDENT BEHAVIOR

When Administrator 6 first became principal of his middle school, he had some students whose behaviors were extremely challenging; many of them were in gangs. He used the behavior support plan that was already in place to mitigate their behaviors. Admittedly, many students were so entrenched in their behaviors that the best he could initially do was minimize their inappropriate choices. He placed approximately ten students into the self-contained environment with a teacher and IA to minimize their disruption. This particular group of boys understood expectations and was appropriate in a one-on-one situation.

However, when they were with their buddies in a group in the hallway or classroom, they wanted to show off for their friends. For instance, one student who was in the administrator's office for inappropriate behavior had a respectful conversation and the issue was resolved. Just moments later, this very same student was in the hallway declaring to his friends that he had really told off the principal. The perception of the student was that announcing he had stood up and confronted the principal enabled him to save face.

The following year, Administrator 6 was able to divide this group of challenging students among the various co-teaching classrooms for all subjects except mathematics. The mathematics teacher was so strong that she was able to address their behaviors. One lesson Administrator 6 admits to learning was placing students with extreme behaviors with teachers who are new to education is ill-advised. "They are often not equipped to handle situations that are extreme even with a co-teacher present."

Once that group of boys moved on, subsequent behavioral groups had more successful outcomes. Administrator 6 emphasizes that students with behavior problems are often very capable academically; they just feel compelled to act out for their friends. Another strategy that worked for these students was allowing them to participate in a behavior support program, which helped them learn to cope when they felt agitated. The behavior support program allowed them to obtain social skills instruction that was applicable to their situation and that could be immediately implemented.

INCLUSION'S IMPACT

Although Administrator 6 occasionally loses sleep worrying about issues such as how the first day of school is going to go, he mostly has confidence in people and students and that there will be improvements. He has established expectations of people and understands they are either going to live up to them or not, but if they seek him out, he will help them meet their potential. He believes that the work that proactively occurs in the front end pays dividends in the long run, so stressing over what might be is too energy zapping.

Administrator 6 believes inclusion practices have had a positive impact on his exceptional students because everyone involved has become more accepting of each other's differences. "One of the seven habits of effective teens is synergy, where students work together in a group to create a better product than can be created by themselves." Exceptional students are now "students," not "the exceptional students" or "from the exceptional class" or "the exceptional group." People see them as being part of the school.

He believes inclusion has had a neutral academic impact on general education students. While the exceptional students have benefited from being included, the general education students have not suffered, "which is why I say the impact has been academically neutral." From a social aspect, inclusion has been very positive because students have had to learn to work with a diverse group of people. Synergy allows students to work in a team to accomplish a goal.

For general educators, inclusion has been positive because they have learned certain aspects about exceptional students that they didn't previously know before being involved in the co-teaching model. Similarly, special educators have enjoyed inclusion because they didn't know certain aspects of the content that was taught. Administrator 6 notes he was fortunate to have special educators who were certified in both exceptional programs as well as in their content area, so certification was not an issue—a real blessing.

SOUTHEAST REGION TALKING POINTS

Procedures

- Focus on student growth.
- Remediate learning gaps (rather than label) economically disadvantaged students.
- Provide opportunities for movement; an energetic student is not necessarily ADHD.
- Honor students' individual needs; some students do well in small settings while others do not.
- Rotate co-teaching teams annually to prevent burnout.
- Place instructional aides in as many general education classes as possible, ensuring they are supporting the neediest students.

Inclusive Buy-In Strategies

- Provide training regarding inclusion, working with behavioral disordered students and differentiated instruction.
- Implement co-teaching; it's research-based and provides the most favorable outcomes.
- Use baseline data to show teachers where their students are performing thus delineating exactly what skill(s) needs to be improved.
- Ask how teachers would want instruction provided for their child if a disability was present.
- Evoke faculty emotions with questions such as, "Are you ever tired of learning one of ours students has dropped out?" and follow up with "What do you see as a solution?"
- Adopt a leadership program such as "The 7 Habits of Highly Effective Teens" and train everybody, both students and staff.
- Permit concerns to be verbalized, thus prompting discussion.
- Empower staff by building teacher-developed programs from the bottom up.
- Transition to inclusive strategies slowly, i.e., starting with partner volunteers.
- Consider blocking periods so targeted academic remediation can occur.

- Check in with teachers periodically to determine and meet needs.
- Provide research-based results-driven software to support content.
- Invite district personnel to present information regarding how inclusion should look.
- Apply for grants to promote inclusion through strategies such as universal design (UD).
- Incentivize teachers to implement inclusion by providing perks such as SMART Boards (bought with grant money).
- Attempt to schedule exceptional students only in co-taught classrooms for reading and mathematics classes for proper support unless the student is high functioning or the teacher is skilled.
- Honor the continuum of services.
- Reorganize teacher or student schedules as the situation warrants.

Sharing Your Vision

- Start the year by describing goals that are built from last year's accomplishments.
- Readdress your vision throughout the year.
- Meet with team leaders who will convey information to their group.
- Email meaningful articles or information to staff.
- Remind teachers that they may be the only fair and consistent person in a challenging student's life.
- Portray inclusion as an opportunity for a diverse student population to have the ability to be exposed to the same information.

Standardized Tests

- Use data obtained through assessments to determine if any learning is occurring.
- Consider success as not just a product of the skill set a student has when he enters the classroom but what is done for the child when present.
- Determine how successful teachers are moving their students in a positive direction so their strategies can be emulated.
- Take advantage of RTT opportunities to earn funds for supplies and resources.
- Douse current frustrations with testing requirements by understanding they will evolve and improve with time.

Teacher Evaluations

- Measure the skill of a teacher via student growth.

Parent Communication

- Procure a phone-calling system that automatically sends messages or announcements.
- Establish a day of the week for parents to expect correspondence such as "Wednesday's Folders."

Addressing Challenging Student Behavior

- Divide challenging students among the various co-teaching classrooms.
- Refrain from placing students with extreme behaviors with teachers who are new to education.
- Provide a behavior support or social skill program that is applicable to the students' situation that can be immediately implemented.

Chapter Six

Administrator 7: Northeast Region

Recently retired, Administrator 7 entered education in the northeast region as a Junior Reserve Officer Training Corps (JROTC) instructor and held this position for about seven-and-a-half years. When he began teaching he knew nothing about special education, but he gained valuable information by working with exceptional students who required accommodations and modifications. With 28 percent of the students in his classes qualifying for special education services, Administrator 7 quickly realized many of the individual education plan (IEP) goals and accommodations his students had seemed unrelated to what they needed. He learned that special educators were able to plug in choices from a drop-down menu in their automated system. The options chosen often did not meet the needs of the student.

To counter poorly written accommodations, Administrator 7 attempted to ascertain what a child really needed and created his own list that appropriately supported each student within the context of his classroom. "Most of the students were extremely receptive to the supports I provided." As time passed, he learned more about IEPs, their requirements and how to better support included students.

For the next five years, Administrator 7 worked at the district office as the director of JROTC. He continued to advocate for the placement of special education students into the JROTC program and military science classes because he recognized these courses gave special education students the opportunity to thrive in places where they had never before been successful. While serving as the director of military programs, he became interested in educational leadership and administration, subsequently obtaining his doctorate and principal's certification. Although included students were discussed throughout different segments of his other coursework, he recalls two courses that helped him better understand exceptional students' needs and how to support them. One was his educational law class and the second was a class that specifically discussed inclusion. He found the information helpful and applicable. "I wish I had been exposed to even more information because I didn't know enough."

Promptly after receiving his administrator's certification, Administrator 7 was asked to fill an opening in a school that desperately needed an assistant principal. Almost every one of the 1,000 students was economically disadvantaged, about 16 percent of the students were on IEPs and test scores were flat in the bottom 5th percentile. Shortly after the school year began, Administrator 7 found that the student population in general was out of control. Moreover, the prior principal had "warehoused" every special education student in one hallway with the exception of the emotionally disturbed students who were in the basement. "Students with disabilities already feel like they lack abilities; they need to be made to feel like they are capable." To counter this situation, Administrator 7 reviewed each student's individual aptitudes to determine the best way to reintegrate them into the general education environment.

Administrator 7 describes inclusion as the practice of placing students with teachers who have the skills and talents to educate them so they will become functioning, productive members of society. To transition his school from exclusion to inclusion, he worked with the roster chair to rewrite schedules and place students in classrooms that were implementing the collaborative group model. For example, he had two autistic support classes that consisted of some of the "kindest, nicest children I have ever met." Administrator 7 placed some of these students in the JROTC program where they "absolutely adored it." Therefore, students who had gone through most of their lives with very little academic support were suddenly privy to field trips, parades and the opportunity to wear a uniform that meant they were part of the group.

Every effort was made to ensure no one teacher was overloaded. This was accomplished by leveling class loads and thoughtfully placing students with teachers that had a reputation for being willing, patient and capable of helping each student grow. During this time Administrator 7 realized that teachers who were newer to the field of education were more amenable to working with students with disabilities than the more experienced teachers, at least in his district. Newer teachers were also more likely to use technology to support students' needs. Administrator 7 admits he gets angry when students don't receive what they should be given. "There are laws that require certain supports for the good of the student, for the good of the human being. The laws require actions that are common sense."

STRUCTURING INCLUSIVE CLASSROOMS

Collaborative groups enabled all students, particularly those who had excess energy, to work in one area for a brief period of time then move to another activity. Combined with technology, the students remained engaged and acquired the joy of learning. For example, a group of students might perform research on the computer for fifteen minutes, create a poster during the next fifteen minutes, and then participate in a brief presentation the final fifteen minutes.

Collaborative learning also enabled students to respond better to their peers, which reinforced learning and permitted opportunities for teachers to learn from their students instead of engaging in direct instruction. In the JROTC environment, collaborative learning meant classes began with an icebreaker, there would be brief instruction, then students would work as a group, and lastly there would be a presentation. Initially resistant to this foreign idea of "collaboration," Administrator 7 became a convert because "the students learned so much more, had such a good time and I enjoyed learning from them."

To support inclusive collaborative classrooms, inclusion training was provided by the principal and Administrator 7 arranged for restorative practices training. The restorative practices educational approach involves developing school policies and procedures that mitigate inappropriate behaviors from occurring in the classroom or on the school campus. Practices include conversations, enquiry, mediation and conferences. The goal is to help pupils learn how to describe their feelings, listen to the other party's point of view, arrive at a mutually agreed upon solution and move forward without holding a grudge. Ultimately, students understand the consequences of inappropriate behavior and therefore choose appropriate alternatives.

To support students in mathematics, the Study Island software program was utilized. As noted in Administrators 4 and 5's Rocky Mountain district, Study Island is a web-based program customized to help students meet the standards in their state. A supplemental tool, the mini-lessons provide instant feedback. For example, correct answers result in a yellow star appearing; wrong answers result in detailed explanations and prompts that assist the student. Study Island is adaptable (the teacher can select specific content and the number of questions to be completed) and goal oriented (the teacher can select the percent correct that constitutes mastery). It also provides remediation (incorrect answers result in a student being cycled down to a lower level until they demonstrate mastery at the more basic level).

Achieve 3000 was a software program used in Administrator 7's science and social studies classrooms. An educational website designed to assist every subgroup in a school (English language learners, exceptional, general education and gifted students), Achieve 3000 integrates technology to support the classroom syllabus. The program assesses a student's reading level and then provides articles that are tailored to their reading ability. For example, students might be reading about amphibians. Each student is able to find an article that can be read at their individual reading ability level.

Thus, students were reading the same content information, but it was presented at a level that was enjoyable and clear for each individual. Students who were next to each other in the computer lab did not know if their neighbor had a higher or lower reading ability than themselves because they had the same pictures and were reading text. Faculty had access to various reports that allowed them to determine if their students were on task and how much of the material was understood. The result was that several students improved their reading scores two grade levels in one year and some students improved as much as four grade levels in one year. "However, the largest benefit was that students enjoyed reading and learning."

COLLABORATION

After serving as an assistant principal for two years, Administrator 7 became principal of two different cyber schools in which he worked with over 900 students from all over his state. Approximately 12 percent of the attendees had a disability. In both the brick-and-mortar school and the cyber school, he had co-teaching teams that were structured into "academies." In an academy, a social studies teacher might work with an English and mathematics teacher; lesson plans were developed to ensure there was learning across the curriculum. For instance, the English teacher might support the social studies teacher's lesson by helping students complete research. The mathematics teacher might help support the lesson by having students determine how much higher one mountain was than another or the distance between cities.

All content teachers, including those in elective classes, incorporated mathematics in their instruction. The goal was for students to understand there was a mathematical component present outside of the mathematics classroom; math concepts can be applied in many facets of life. This ultimately helped students not hate math; instead, students found math enjoyable.

Administrator 7 asserts that finding time to collaborate was easiest in the cyber school environment. To eke out time in the brick-and-mortar school, teachers who were cooperating with each other would have their classes scheduled back-to-back. That is, a student might navigate from science to English where the cooperating team teacher would help with constructing a research paper that coincided with the content being studied in science. Additional collaborative opportunities occurred during a common prep time, usually made possible by scheduling students into elective classes. Extra prep time was occasionally scheduled for teachers to create lesson plans and post grades, made possible by bringing in personnel to cover classes. "The principal was very good with finding extra money to bring in a relief teacher."

Conversely, in the cyber school, teachers usually worked in the building three days a week and from home up to two days a week. When in the office, they would have grade- or content-level meetings that had been scheduled prior to the meeting time. This was easily effected because teachers were in their work area and could simply turn their chair around and be at a table in the center of the room. Additionally, there were conference rooms within the building that could be utilized. Meetings could also occur via the Elluminate Live! Program that permitted teachers to call in, talk, post pictures, write on electronic whiteboards and upload materials. "The live classrooms were very effective."

There was usually at least one core content teacher for each grade level, sometimes more. On the other hand, two English teachers might service the four high school grade levels. All elective courses had an academic component. To monitor the physical activity component of physical education, students wore an electronic monitoring device that recorded their heart rate and subsequently sent the data to their teacher's computer. Moreover, students had the option to obtain physical education credit by enrolling in community classes such as karate or bowling. A signed form from their instructor indicating they had participated as evidenced by their logs resulted in earned credit for the class. The logs were usually scanned to the teachers electronically. "Although this was not a perfect system it worked quite well."

Administrator 7 muses that he had to walk the halls in a brick-and-mortar school in order to gather information regarding what his teachers and students were doing. In his cyber school, he was able to determine who was in class and how well they were doing by looking at his screen. Live classrooms ran from 8 a.m. to 8 p.m. Teachers had staggered schedules that ensured there was always one content teacher available. Those who had night hours would not enter the virtual classroom until noon and would remain until 8 p.m.

As a result, students could access their work at any time twenty-four hours a day, seven days per week and could obtain assistance from their teacher between 8 a.m. and 8 p.m. during the regular school week. If they needed specific help, they could electronically raise their hands by pressing a button on their keyboard that caused the teacher's computer to emit a noise. Teachers could then turn on their webcam and verbally speak with the student, provide visual examples and upload additional examples to assist with the learning. An electronic resource room was also available for students who needed remedial or resource support from a special educator. Students had the option to toggle between regular instruction and resource support as needed.

In his cyber school, Administrator 7's staff wrote gifted individual education plans (GIEPs) for students who qualified. To ensure GIEPs were written well, he sent one of his teachers to receive specialized training. To support gifted students' abilities, teachers created projects that required more complex thinking (such as judging the value of various objects rather than listing them) in addition to the normal requirements of the lesson. Administrator 7 opines that parents of gifted students often want to micromanage the GIEP process, believing their child is a virtuoso. (He notes that he never saw GIEPs implemented in a brick-and-mortar school.)

CHALLENGES IMPLEMENTING INCLUSION

Administrator 7 recognizes having more staff would have enabled him to implement his inclusive programs more effectively. Also, in his brick-and-mortar school there were some resistant senior staff members who were unhappy when classes were restructured to an inclusive model; newer staff members were more accepting and flexible. Second, he could have used more parental support. He likens parent involvement to the Bell curve.

On one end there are parents who are absolutely amazing, willing to do anything asked who are completely committed to their child. On the other end there are parents who are completely uninvolved to the point of negligence. "It was shameful. Parents wouldn't show up for their child's IEP meeting, wouldn't return forms and would claim they never received any paperwork." The bulk of parents were between these two extremes.

Third, he did not have enough instructional aides (IAs) in the resource environment and those he had "were usually not up to the task." Most of them lacked the training, interest, caring and patience required to encourage exceptional students to be all they can be. On the other hand, Administrator 7 recalls a teacher who had been an IA prior to obtaining her certification who was "wonderful. I did not know her as an IA but imagine she was absolutely outstanding."

CYBER SCHOOL

Administrator 7 admits to experiencing a large learning curve when he initially became the principal of a virtual school. Originally, the special education coordinator was the only special education teacher. She would move around to the different general education classes and support the exceptional students, which was very productive. The program grew and eventually there were four special educators, one who taught each content area and spent approximately 25 percent of their time working with special education students. IAs also provided support in the general education environment.

To hold IEP meetings in his cyber school environment, every teacher who worked with the exceptional student was present, which went above and beyond IDEA's requirement of having only one general educator present. Sometimes participation was electronic but it was very beneficial to have every teacher present. "Having every teacher present in a brick-and-mortar school was a bit more challenging."

When student progress in a brick-and-mortar school is compared to progress in a cyber-school, Administrator 7 asserts students made greater progress in the cyber school environment. He theorizes that negative factors in the inner-city brick-and-mortar school where he worked were the size of the school that housed 1,000 students and the lack of commitment and dedication from the teachers. There were many other distractors including violence, fires being set and the lack of instructional materials. The cyber-school was much smaller with only 500 students in the high school. Also, Administrator 7 lived by the creed, "Students don't care how much you know, they want to know how much you care." He did not have unions dictating whether or not he had the authority to hire or retain teachers if they did not abide by that creed in the cyber school.

As a result, several students did amazingly well in the cyber environment. He credits the success of many inner-city students to his special education teacher who understood how to work with both the student and their parents. "She was relentless and did not give up." He recalls one young man who began the year reading at the kindergarten level and completed the year reading at the second grade level. Similarly, his brother improved his reading four grade levels in one year. "These students truly earned their grades."

This brings Administrator 7 to another important observation. In the brick-and-mortar school, students were often "given" grades. In the cyber school environment, students had to earn their grades. Performance could not be faked because there was an electronic record. If students struggled, teachers worked with them until they understood the concept, which largely mitigated "learned helplessness." Furthermore, in the cyber environment, all teachers were offered a financial bonus for student improvement, which was determined by growth as demonstrated by test scores.

ANCILLARY SERVICES IN A CYBER ENVIRONMENT

Some students in a virtual environment still require ancillary services such as occupational therapy (OT), physical therapy (PT) or speech language services. Therapists were contracted and paid for by the school. In his state, 80 percent of the cyber school per capita costs comes from the student's home district. Additionally, almost 100 percent of the cost to support a special education student was received to provide the services needed. "Funding is a challenge in a cyber school and often requires individuals to wear more than one hat."

Obtaining speech language services was a challenge that surfaced more recently. Administrator 7 went to such great lengths to support his students that he reached out to a company in Canada that provided services online, "but I was most unimpressed. Services were not geared to high school level students." Conversely, contracted services for OT and PT and psychology worked out rather well.

STANDARDIZED TESTS

Administrator 7 believes it is very difficult to accurately evaluate exceptional students when they do not receive accommodations commensurate with their respective present levels of performance or what is delineated on the IEP. He does believe students should be evaluated; however, the way this is currently happening has no value. To ask students to perform at grade level without proper content accommodations "is flat wrong." He therefore believes the time could be better spent elsewhere. One way students could demonstrate whether or not they are capable of testing is by evaluating them with a classroom diagnostic tool (CDT).

The CDTs could be used to evaluate students at various academic levels thereby identifying a student's strengths and areas that need remediation. For example, if a student reads at the fifth grade level, he could take the fifth grade test to demonstrate proficiency. "I am just thinking out loud, but this would be much more appropriate than requiring every student to take a test at the eleventh grade level regardless of who they are or what their abilities were when they registered." Requiring all students (refugee, cognitively impaired, former inmates, gifted) to take the same test regardless of their abilities or experiences does not accurately indicate what the teachers or students can do. A student can move only so far in a year; administering a blanket assessment without considering the individual's "story" or disregarding baseline data does not accurately measure growth. "Students who are cognitively impaired should not be required to take the same test as their gifted peers."

Administrator 7 notes that in the cyber (and brick-and-mortar) environment, tests are now available online. Prior to this, students had to take a pencil and paper test in a location within two hours of their home; attendance was required. One issue with the current online test is the need to have sufficient bandwidth. To ensure such, a location would have had to been rented although some cyber schools have been able to negotiate space with their local university. Due to bandwidth and other technological concerns, Administrator 7 administered his test via pencil and paper.

COMMON CORE STATE STANDARD

Administrator 7 is in favor of implementing the Common Core State Standards and calls the concept "an excellent idea." However, he does not believe it is realistic. He notes that states currently do not have a common assessment because no state wants to be ranked in the bottom percentile on statewide testing. He maintains educators should work toward the same goals to avoid "dumbing down" the curriculum and to better prepare students to compete globally. He surmises national exit testing would ensure students have met expectations.

However, as a confederation of fifty states, the Constitution permits each state to exercise their individual conscience. This is evidenced by each state having its own traffic, marriage and drug laws. Similarly, teachers from one state are not considered credentialed in another state; if a teacher moves they are required to take an exam to demonstrate they have the knowledge skills and abilities to perform their duties. "Taking one national test seems like a smart decision. However, moving to a national standard would expose states that are not performing well as compared to other states and no state leader wants to face that possibility."

INCLUSION'S IMPACT

Administrator 7 believes the benefit of implementing an inclusion model is that special education students realize they are capable of performing academically and don't need to be coddled. Talking to students, getting to know them by asking them what they need or what their struggles are can prove to be enlightening. Providing an opportunity for exceptional students to be educated with their general education peers helps their classmates learn acceptance. Data shows test scores, grades and attendance improve while inappropriate behavior and suspensions decrease because students have a reason to go to class. "They aren't being pigeonholed in some nasty hallway or a classroom that is either freezing or overheated."

Administrator 7 emphasizes that people are not all the same. However, just because someone is not going to be a brain surgeon does not mean that person cannot be a pilot or an accountant. People learn differently so teachers need to have inclusion classrooms that provide everything that students need. Truly differentiating takes a special type of educator.

This administrator entered the field of education believing when students are included with their general education peers their teachers must water down the curriculum to meet the needs of exceptional students while disregarding the needs of general education students. Once he worked with exceptional students and saw the results he became a convert. "I saw how beneficial inclusion is for everyone. If one gets away from the mentality of 'chalk and talk' the student is given more opportunities to be 'doing.' In any class there are varying levels of ability that the teacher has to recognize. The way the standard is met can and should be individualized for each student."

NORTHEAST REGION TALKING POINTS

Procedures

- Rewrite IEP goals if they do not accurately address a student's current needs.
- Avoid using computerized drop down menu choices that provide objectives unrelated to the goal.
- Provide opportunities for struggling students to participate in courses in which they can experience success.
- Place students with teachers who have the skills and talents to educate them.
- Implement the collaborative group model to keep students engaged.
- Ensure "good" teachers are not overloaded with challenging students; level classes.
- Offer technology to support students' needs.

Structuring Inclusive Classrooms

- Structure classrooms into collaborative groups permitting students to alternate activities.
- Implement student-led classroom strategies.
- Mitigate inappropriate behaviors by training teachers and students in the restorative practices educational approach.
- Purchase and train teachers to use software programs such as Study Island and Achieve 3000.

Collaboration

- Structure co-teaching teams into "academies" to ensure learning occurs across the curriculum.
- Incorporate content from different courses into your class, i.e., social studies teachers can include math or science concepts into their discussion.
- Schedule students in back-to-back classes of cooperating teachers, i.e., students leave science and go to English to conduct their research and write a report.

- Provide a common prep time for collaborating teachers by scheduling students into electives.
- Bring in substitute teachers or other personnel to occasionally cover a class, which allows collaborating teachers to attend workshops and create lesson or unit plans.
- Preschedule grade- or content-level meetings.
- Consult via the Elluminate Live! Program.
- Create gifted IEPs to support advanced students.

Cyber School

- Permit students to enroll in community classes such as karate or bowling to earn physical education credits.
- Expect every teacher who works with an exceptional student to attend IEP meetings either in person or electronically.
- Purchase software that remediates gaps and permits a student to move forward once content is mastered.
- Check electronic data frequently to assess student progress.
- Contract ancillary services.

Standardized Tests

- Compare on-line testing options and consider if paper-and-pencil or online testing is better for your population of students.
- Negotiate with a local university if more computer space or larger band-width is needed.

Inclusion's Impact

- Exceptional students realize they are capable of performing academically and don't need to be coddled.
- Data shows test scores, grades and attendance improve.
- Data shows inappropriate behaviors and suspensions decrease.
- Students have more opportunities to be "doing."

Chapter Seven

Administrator 8: Midwest Region

Administrator 8 attended a university in the southeast where she obtained both her bachelor's and master's degrees in speech language pathology and audiology. She was initially employed for four years on a federal project during which time her primary responsibility was to observe teacher-student communication in the classroom for the purpose of enhancing communication skills for cognitively disabled (CD) students. The following year she was a speech language pathologist (SLP) in a K–12 school district. She then worked for one year in a private speech language clinic before moving to the northeast where she worked as a state consultant performing evaluations and designing programs for CD children in school systems and CD adults in group homes and day services centers.

Four years later, Administrator 8 moved to the Midwest region and worked for a regional services center for the next twenty-five years. The regional services centers serve as a liaison between the State Department of Public Instruction and the school districts. Initially an SLP support person, she transitioned into the position of M-Team Reviewer, responsible for maintaining special education paperwork in various school districts. She followed that position by becoming an assistant director and then a director of special education for the service center in a variety of rural school districts. Her final three years in education were spent as a director of special education for a comprehensive school district that has a population of 1,800 students. Approximately 200 of those students (11 percent) have a disability. Although the elementary school students recently tested in the bottom half of the state, both the middle and high schools tested in the top 25th percentile.

Administrator 8 is very cognizant of disproportionality issues. In the past, well-intentioned special educators had a tendency to misidentify English language learners (ELLs) as exceptional students with the virtuous intention of providing accommodations to help them. To counter this, her district hired an ELL teacher for each school (elementary, middle and high school) to work with these students both in resource rooms and in the classroom. Consequently, faculty members are less frequently misidentifying ELL students as disabled because they are aware that a certified staff member is available to assist them.

Administrator 8 notes that she began her career with what was then called "trainable mentally retarded" children who were taught in a school completely segregated from their peers (these students are currently called "cognitively disabled," "cognitively impaired" or "intellectually disabled"). Exceptional students who were higher functioning were segregated most of their day via placement in resource rooms. Although they received skill work that was most relevant to them, they were not exposed to the general curriculum and were excluded from opportunities to interact socially. For example, there was a classroom teacher who, at the beginning of the school year, would have a party for the students she had taught the previous year. The exceptional students always asked if they were supposed to go; they weren't sure if they were to attend because they had been pulled out of class so often to receive their special education services. Socially, these students were not even sure if they were really part of this regular education classroom, "which is very telling about how they felt about themselves."

To learn about inclusion, Administrator 8 attended an Association of Supervision and Curriculum Development annual convention with a curriculum and instruction (C&I) co-worker where Dr. Marilyn Friend was presenting. She attended a "Train the Trainer" conference for a day, which is where she initially received Dr. Friend's inclusion/co-teaching resources. This sparked her interest in co-teaching, so she followed up in seeking more information regarding co-teaching strategies. Administrator 8 and her C&I coworker created a workshop and trained faculty in a variety of school districts. "It was good to work with my C&I colleague because I knew the special education piece and she knew the general education curriculum and instruction piece. One benefit from developing our workshop together was that it enabled us to demonstrate to the co-teaching teams how two people could work together to blend these areas."

THE EVOLUTION OF INCLUSION

To help teachers transition to inclusion, multiple two-day workshops describing the co-teaching model were held by Administrator 8 and her C&I colleague. They presented material regarding basic information about how people work together in general, which segued into how two teachers can work in a classroom together. Activities with the staff included identifying annoyances, rules about discipline, classroom organization and similar items so that each teacher could share their philosophies and be able to arrive at a common consensus of how their unified class should be managed. Other discussions involved commonalities and how responsibilities would be divided and shared.

Co-teaching approaches include:

- one teach, one observe (where one co-teacher leads the lesson while the other co-teacher makes detailed observations of students engaged in the learning process);
- one teach, one drift (where one co-teacher takes primary responsibility to lead the lesson while the other co-teacher circulates around the room assisting students when needed);
- station teaching (where both content and students are divided between stations, and students rotate from one co-teacher's station to another);
- parallel teaching (where both co-teachers instruct the same information, but they divide the class into two groups and conduct the lessons simultaneously);
- alternative teaching (where one co-teacher completes a planned lesson with a large group while the other co-teacher completes an alternative lesson or the same lesson taught at a different level); and
- team teaching (where both co-teachers deliver instruction simultaneously, and instruction becomes more than turn taking).

To further support these teams, specialists provide training throughout the year. For example, a hearing and vision impaired teacher works directly in the classroom with students in their specific areas of disability. They then consult with teachers one to three days per week regarding specific interventions that will assist the child. Similarly, an autism specialist consults with the school district one day per week.

All elementary students (except the most severe) are currently educated all day in the general education classroom through the co-teaching model, defined as classrooms being staffed with one full-time certified general and one certified special education teacher as well as a special education instructional aide (IA). At the middle school, there are some co-taught classes, specifically in reading and mathematics. Approximately one-third of the students in a co-taught classroom have a disability and two-thirds of the students do not. If the ratio exceeds 1:2 special to general education students, more support is provided or classes are leveled by moving students. "We have evolved from complete segregation and providing special educational services in a pull-out model to educating and servicing all students together as much as possible."

When Administrator 8 first began to work at her current district, all of the emotional behavioral disordered (EBD) and CD students were bussed out of the district to programs in other school districts. In approximately 2003, a new superintendent was hired who worked with Administrator 8 to bring these students back to their home district. This was followed by gradually changing the structural framework so services could be provided through a co-teaching model. Initially, teachers were very leery of the inclusion concept. Administrator 8 states this is understandable; since the 1970s teachers were led to believe that only special educators had the skills to accommodate exceptional students.

General educators, therefore, became dependent on special educators to provide services to exceptional students. As time passed and they rarely interacted with special education students, their opinion evolved to believe they were unqualified to adequately support students with a disability. Their perspective was, "You work with disabled students because I am incapable of doing so, but that's okay because I have plenty to do." Now they are told, "You do have the skill set and we are going to help you hone those skills as we move all but the most severe special education students back into your classroom."

Recognizing many general educators felt hesitant and incompetent, initial co-teaching teams were created by matching general education volunteers with their special education colleagues. Although many general educators became more willing to try, there were teachers who thought (and still think) they should not have to deal with special education students "because that is someone else's job."

As the inclusion model was being implemented, it became clear that two populations of students would require special attention—the EBD and autism spectrum disordered (ASD) students. EBD students have been particularly challenging. "Even with two teachers in a classroom, it only takes just one student's explosive behavior to disrupt the learning of the other twenty-five students." To successfully address these episodes, teachers have restructured their classroom, "which is no small task." Moreover, the special educator occasionally works with the EBD student for part of the day outside of the classroom and returns when the student has decompressed and is able to act appropriately.

Thus far, ASD students in Administrator 8's district have been mostly higher functioning and are fully included at the elementary level with weekly consultation provided to staff by a specialist from the regional services center. At the middle school where they are in a co-taught classroom, there is a resource period for them to complete tasks or receive remediation. At the high school level there are no co-taught classrooms; students attend a resource study hall or take resource classes to give them extra time to complete their work and support learning gaps. Classroom teachers at the middle school and high school are also are supported by the regional services autism specialist who consults with them one day per week. The specialist observes a student for a couple of hours and then provides ideas, materials and feedback. This specialist also organizes workshops, after school trainings with small groups presenting on in-service days in the district for a wider variety of staff.

TRAINING AND COLLABORATION

The initial co-teaching training was made possible by providing training during the summer or by placing substitute teachers in classrooms for two days, enabling certified teachers to attend the workshop. As the year progressed, substitute teachers were brought in periodically so the teams could be further trained. Collaboration time for all teachers currently occurs during "late start" every Wednesday morning. Co-teachers also have daily common planning time during their "prep."

Co-teaching teams are also provided with a substitute teacher for a half-day each quarter for the purpose of long range planning for the next quarter. Furthermore, elementary education teachers can collaborate while students are in art, music and physical education. "We really worked on providing adequate planning time because we knew without it co-teaching doesn't work; teams have to be able to plan together. Administrators can't expect them to do all their planning 'on the fly' or on their own time."

As time went by and Administrator 8 was actively supporting the co-teaching inclusion process, teachers slowly became more familiar and comfortable with the concept. She surmises that permitting teachers to volunteer to be a co-teaching member (that is, no one was told they had to team up with someone else) and providing multiple supports are important factors that helped the process move forward. The result was the first year ended with only one co-teaching team disbanding due to a personality conflict. Otherwise, the other teams liked working with each other and became more at ease and effective. After four years elapsed, one general educator asked to not co-teach after experiencing a particularly difficult year with challenging students. However, another teacher immediately volunteered to step into the position and the new team worked well together over the next two years.

Administrator 8 notes many of the faculty members in her district are very forward thinking and seek out the best strategies to support their students. "Asking for volunteers and providing classroom supports and resources set teachers up for success." Furthermore, teachers became great partners. "At the end of the second year, a newspaper reporter did a story on co-teaching and asked students how they liked being in a co-teaching classroom. One student responded that he liked it, but he couldn't get away with anything because if one teacher didn't catch him doing something wrong the other did—there was someone always watching him."

Administrator 8 states the biggest challenge she faced when desiring to smoothly transition her schools into an inclusive environment was determining how co-teaching teams would be created. She found that not forcing teachers to be on a team but letting them volunteer while ensuring they received adequate support and planning time was effective. She emphasizes that properly scheduling students is imperative and this only occurs as a result of a supportive administration as exemplified by her principals. One elementary principal first schedules "specials" for the students in the co-taught classrooms, which in turn ensures these occur at a time teachers can co-plan. This was also challenging during the initial stages of co-teaching when one special education teacher co-taught at two grade levels, one classroom in the morning and one in the afternoon. The elementary principal scheduled math and reading at opposite times of the day for those two classrooms so that the special education teacher could be in the classrooms at both grade levels during reading and math instruction.

SUBLIMINAL MESSAGES

The first year, one third-grade classroom was used as a "pilot" to determine how co-teaching would work; the next year an inclusion co-teaching classroom existed at every grade level. That first year, the third grade classroom completed their unit on the rainforest. Students, including the special education students, thoroughly enjoyed the unit, decorating their classroom so that it became a rain forest—at least to the extent this can happen with paper and tissue. In previous years, special education students were removed from the class during that unit due to concerns that they could not understand the vocabulary or understand more complex concepts. The first year of co-teaching, one of the special education students scored the highest grade on the test.

> When we as adults determine something is too difficult and students can't do it, we automatically exclude them from having the opportunity to try. Once co-teaching occurred, we learned we were wrong and some exceptional students are very capable. This was a good lesson for us. We thought our intentions were pure and we were doing the right thing for the student by protecting them from the stress of effort. We excluded them when we shouldn't have—just like we exclude general educators from working with special education students under the assumption they can't.

Administrator 8 notes this "you can't" attitude also spills over into IEP meetings. When students are asked what they need, the response often is, "I don't know, you're the teacher—you're supposed to tell me what I should be doing." Interestingly, the greatest success with student-led IEPs is occurring with the CD students because their teacher has been very involved in getting this to happen. Consequently, CD students create PowerPoint presentations about themselves and what they are doing in education (present levels of academic achievement and functional performance). Having the technological tools to describe themselves is wonderful. Sadly, many high school students don't know how to self-advocate during IEPs (or any other time) because adults have always done everything for them.

INSTRUCTIONAL AIDES

Although Administrator 8 has experienced a few situations in which instructional aides have had to be replaced, they "are usually quite exceptional." Each co-taught classroom has a full-time IA. They work individually with students, perform station teaching functions (highly supervised), sit near a student with behavior issues (or remove the student to work without peripheral distractions), or take a group of students to assist them on skill work. At the elementary level, an IA is in each classroom for a couple of hours each day and full-time in a co-taught classroom. They also accompany students to their elective classes if this support is needed.

Furthermore, IAs rotate through the workroom to ensure copies are made and tasks such as cutting shapes for bulletin boards or laminating items occurs. At the middle school level, each special educator has a full-time aide. The teacher determines the classroom where the IA will be most needed. Sometimes the IA is the third adult in a co-taught math class or may be placed in a science classroom where several special education students are placed but there is no certified special educator. Other times the IA might be supervising a study hall.

At the high school level, students are included in all content classes (there are no co-taught classes) and an aide might be present, depending on the need. Exceptional students often receive support in a study hall that is staffed by two special education aides. Thus, the IA who is in the history class with students is able to assist them in study hall because she knows what the teacher covered in class and what the expectations of the assignment are. In the meantime, the special educator teaches a resource level basic skills class, helping students improve basic concept abilities. For example, the special education math teacher might teach consumer math that conveys concepts and applications the student does not receive in algebra. Students receive elective credits for resource classes and content credits from the teacher who is credentialed to teach the subject.

DATA

Administrator 8 initially saw improvement in state test scores correlated with the students who were included with their general education peers in co-taught classrooms; however, that growth has leveled off. Even though their test scores are not showing growth, students are performing better on their coursework. Administrator 8 theorizes one of the negatives that might influence scores is that co-teaching teams become comfortable after several years together. The special educator begins to emulate the general educator and no longer addresses the skill deficits to the extent they were before implementing the inclusion model.

Thus, special educators evolve into being more focused on the general curriculum than they are on remediating specific skill deficits or the learning needs of the exceptional students. "On the one hand, students are being exposed to the curriculum; on the other hand they are not having their skill deficits addressed to the extent needed." Time is also a factor in trying to provide both the general curriculum and specific skill deficit remediation.

"In fact, one special educator asked the reading specialist for assistance when teaching reading to a specific student. When the special educator who was hired to support students with a reading disability has to ask the reading specialist for help that is evidence we have moved too far away from our respective roles." This begs the question what special instruction is occurring so the students who are being exposed to the general curriculum are also having their skill deficits addressed. "To address this issue, special educators need to be retrained regarding their role of addressing skill deficits. Our teachers are good; we often have three adults in the classroom with these students, so there is no reason for them not to perform better."

Administrator 8 speculates one reason students aren't performing well on tests might be the absence of prompts like they are afforded when in class. Prompts allow students to focus (or refocus) and formulate ideas after being frozen with no idea on how to move forward. IEPs provide verbal prompts as an accommodation; removing this accommodation from a testing environment is clearly detrimental. "Tests aren't designed to activate the knowledge a student has and allow them to demonstrate this knowledge. The fact that state tests are changing to be based on the Common Core State Standards and moving toward practical application of knowledge is concerning. For many special education students, watching a video, for example, and applying what they observed to solve problem sets is going to be very difficult."

Data shows discipline incidents have declined with special education students. Administrator 8 recalls when all EBD students were housed in one special education self-contained classroom. Their misbehavior was not always brought to the principal's attention because the teachers handled the situation. Now that most of these students are included, general educators who are in co-teaching teams are learning how to better deal with all students' discipline by emulating how special educators address behavioral matters.

Therefore, even though there was an initial spike in behavior issues when EBD students first entered the general education classroom, as time progressed teachers have learned how to work with EBD students' inappropriate behaviors, mitigating the need to write referrals. Furthermore, general educators have extrapolated what they have learned and applied the same strategies to resolve issues with general education students who in the past would have been sent to the office. Behavioral referrals are therefore not occurring as often and student conduct has improved for all students.

STANDARDIZED TESTS

Administrator 8 confesses to "being of two minds" regarding standardized tests. She understands if exceptional students are not tested then educators are erroneously inferring they cannot succeed and they are being given a "pass" by not having to demonstrate knowledge. This would indefensibly absolve the special educator from implementing the general curriculum. "However, the state test as it exists is relatively meaningless for special education students. It does not show what students know in relation to the general education students because they learn and express their learning differently." Exceptional students need prompts or the opportunity to express what they know verbally rather than answering either electronically or with pencil and paper.

Students are overwhelmed with multiple pages of reading followed by a few questions, then several more pages of reading followed by a few questions. This results in exceptional students defaulting to filling in the multiple choice bubble without giving much thought to the content. Telling them they have to do their best while dropping large amounts of information in their lap has no benefit. Good intentions of keeping the bar high but doing so through distorted methods does not provide meaningful information for these students. "We need to be able to hold students accountable, which extends beyond them reaching their IEP goals. But the way this is being done now is not gleaning beneficial information."

Regarding the Common Core State Standards (CCSS), Administrator 8 sees a benefit to specifying what students need to know. Exposing both special and general education students to the information ensures everyone is getting similar instruction. "I like the idea of someone deciding the ten big things everybody needs to know. If a student truly needs special education supports, we are acknowledging that the student does not process information in the same manner as everybody else. Exposure to the same material without limits means special education students are going to struggle to be successful because they learn at a slower pace. Identifying the key items helps resolve this situation."

Administrator 8 recognizes this brings up the all-important issue that moving through material quickly to meet standards means educators are missing opportunities to address gaps and skill deficit areas for special education students. Although it is good to create a guide regarding key items students need to know, it should not be at the expense of what the individual student needs. For instance, to not provide consumer math for exceptional students who need to learn how to balance their checkbook or to miss opportunities to provide other practical content is concerning. Similarly, units such as the rainforest (mentioned above) in which students were so engaged have been eliminated because that information is not on the state test. Furthermore, eliminating opportunities for interesting people to present to students due to lack of time means students might not hear something that has the potential to become a future interest or career for them. "The question is if all of the fun is removed, why will students want to learn?"

ANCILLARY STAFF

When Administrator 8 was an SLP, all therapy was conducted on a pull-out basis. Although this is still the dominant method of providing therapy, the SLP also goes into the classroom more and correlates speech and language with reading, both with articulation when reading words are misread and also with oral language. "If oral language is deficient written language also suffers." Station time exists in the classroom and during this time, the SLP can work on sounds and oral language as part of the reading instruction. More intense drill work without distractions still occurs in a pull-out environment.

Occupational therapy and physical therapy occurs largely on a pull-out basis, but occupational therapists and physical therapists are also beginning to do some work in the classroom. This permits them to integrate their strategies to help the student with the classroom teacher. It is important for teachers to understand that students who are not doing their work are not necessarily defiant. For example, a student might be talking to his classmate or working on an assignment from his book because he is unable to copy from the board. "This can become a cycle of not working that evolves into an inappropriate behavior, which could be avoided if the teacher collaborates with the appropriate therapist and learns how to support the student in the classroom. Many behaviors can be virtually eliminated with good communication when they stem from a skill deficit."

TECHNOLOGY AND RESOURCES

Administrator 8's high school special education math teacher has used Study Island software because many incoming students are working on basic math skills while other students are able to work at the algebraic level. As noted in Administrators 4 and 5 and Administrator 7's discussion, Study Island is a web-based program customized to help students meet the standards in their state. A supplemental tool, the mini-lessons provide instant feedback. For example, correct answers result in a yellow star appearing; wrong answers result in detailed explanations and prompts that assist the student. Study Island is adaptable (the teacher can select specific content and the number of questions to be completed) and goal oriented (the teacher can select the percent correct that constitutes mastery). It also provides remediation (incorrect answers result in a student being cycled down to a lower level until they demonstrate mastery at the more basic level).

The Assessment and Learning in Knowledge Spaces (ALEKS) math program, a web-based assessment and learning system, is currently being used at the high school level and with some students at the middle school level. It uses adaptive questioning to determine what a student knows and doesn't know in a course and then instructs the student on topics the student is most ready to learn. Periodic reassessment occurs to ensure the student retains the topics learned.

Additionally, all students are issued a laptop when they enter high school. They check it back in at the end of the year or keep it for the summer with parent signed permission. If something happens to the computer while in the student's care, they are responsible for the replacement cost. Students continue with the same computer throughout their high school career.

At the elementary level, the general education reading curriculum, LEAD 2, is supplemented with Reading Mastery, Systematic Instruction in Phonological Awareness, Phonics and Sight Words (SIPPS), Sound Partners and Reading A-Z. The students also have iPads, laptops and LearnPads available to use, and each classroom is equipped with a SMART Board. Behavior programs used with special education students at the elementary level include the Second Step Social Skills program and Superflex, a superhero social thinking curriculum. Read 180 was used at the high school level, but it has been phased out because it required two periods to be scheduled back-to-back to cover its three components (computer instruction, direct instruction and independent reading).

INCLUSION'S IMPACT

Administrator 8 believes her district's inclusion practices have had a positive impact on students with disabilities. Even though the test scores are not elevated, students feel better about academics because they believe they have the support that they need and are not getting as frustrated. Socially they perceive they are part of their classroom and they feel less "different." There is less confusion because they aren't pulled into various classrooms every hour.

General education students who may be academically at risk benefit from the inclusion co-teaching model because they have two teachers who present coursework material using different methods. For example, the special educator may present visuals to coincide with the general educator's auditory presentation. Students might also be exposed to alternative procedures to analyze problems because they are receiving instruction from two teachers with different backgrounds and presentation styles. Students also learn compassion from being around others who have a variety of challenges; they learn everyone has strengths and weaknesses. Someone who might not be strong in math could be a strong reader, so one can help the other with what they do well, which helps develop their ability to interact with a diverse group of people.

Inclusion has been both positive and negative for general educators. Positives include co-teaching with someone who can share the joys and converse about the day's difficulties. Skill sets and responsibilities are shared, and working with diverse students helps educators hone their craft. Negatives occur when teachers feel like there has been an intrusion upon their territory. They worked well with their general education students and are uncertain about their ability to be effective with the special education population with whom they have not worked for many years.

Like the general educator, the special educator has been comfortable with their routine in their resource room. Being asked to work with and be responsible for all students in addition to IEP responsibilities while being required to learn the general education curriculum can be daunting. Furthermore, some teachers who thought their resource classroom provided sufficient rigor might realize they have not been teaching grade-level information and feel embarrassed that they do not know some of the content.

When the CD and EBD students were segregated many general educators were saying, "We don't have to work with those students in our classroom." When they were brought back to their home school, parents were initially asking, "What are those students doing in my child's classroom?" On a positive note, as time has progressed both teachers and parents have become much more accepting of the inclusion concept.

MIDWEST REGION TALKING POINTS

Evolution of Inclusion

- Educate yourself and colleagues by attending workshops such as Marilyn Friend's "The Co-Teaching in the Collaborative and Inclusive Classroom."
- Develop faculty workshops with a colleague so co-teaching and collaboration can be modeled.
- Establish initial co-teaching teams through a volunteer process.
- Allow general educators to rotate out of co-teaching responsibilities annually.
- Place IAs into classroom where support is most needed.
- Implement true co-teaching by staffing included classrooms with one full-time general and one full-time special educator as appropriate.
- Pre-plan strategies to address the needs of EBD and ASD students.
- Schedule resource support classes for exceptional students.
- Schedule exceptional students into co-teaching and elective classes first, then schedule other students.
- Have the certified special educator teach a resource class such as consumer math or English so skill gaps can be addressed.

Training and Collaboration

- Incorporate time during initial co-teaching training for teaching teams to discuss their personalities, strengths and weaknesses with teaching partners.
- Help train staff so that students generalize what was learned in one class to another class.
- Permit teachers to have time to develop lesson plans and discuss the division of responsibilities.
- Provide training throughout the year via specialists who work with teachers individually, in small groups or in large in-services.
- Schedule specialists for classroom observations followed by collaboration time with the teacher in which materials ideas and feedback are discussed.
- Hire substitute teachers to cover classes so teachers can attend workshops.
- Employ these substitutes periodically throughout the year for ongoing training.
- Pre-schedule teacher collaboration time on specific days such as "Late Start Wednesdays."
- Enable co-teachers to collaborate during a common prep period.

- Staff classrooms with substitute teachers for a half-day once per quarter so teams can develop long-range plans for the following quarter.

Subliminal Messages

- Convey the belief that every student deserves an opportunity to be included and exposed to information.
- Project the attitude that all students can learn something from an activity or lesson.
- Adopt the perspective that general educators do have the skills to effectively educate exceptional students.
- In-service educators on how exceptional students can be taught to self-advocate during IEP meetings.

Instructional Aides

- Ensure IAs are properly trained and understand their responsibilities and expectations.
- Place IAs in co-taught classrooms as appropriate.
- Help teachers learn how to utilize IAs in classroom stations.
- Seat IAs near students with behavior issues.
- Permit IAs to take students whose behaviors are escalating to a predetermined area where they can safely decompress and/or work.
- Seat an IA with a group of students during group work time.
- Ensure IAs accompany exceptional students to electives as needed.
- Rotate IAs through the workroom to ensure teachers have worksheets copied and items laminated.
- Use two IAs as study hall supervisors.

Data

- Ensure special educators are remediating specific skill deficits and not merely emulating their general education colleagues when in co-taught classrooms.
- Expect initial data to show a spike in discipline issues when first including EBD students.
- Train general educators to imitate strategies their special education colleagues use to respond to EBD students' antics.
- Share data that shows academic gains and discipline reductions.

Common Core State Standards

- Teach key concepts to benefit every student.
- Use the key concepts as a guide remembering that what individuals need varies from student to student.
- Keep learning fun.

Ancillary Staff

- Encourage ancillary staff to observe students in the classroom.
- Follow-up consultations by OTs, PTs, and SLPs should help teachers understand how a student's OI or SLI affects their ability to perform or understand information.
- Allow ancillary staff to work with students during station time.
- Help teachers understand that students who are off-task may not understand directions or may be unable to copy material due to their disability.

Technology and Resources

- Use web-based programs such as Study Island to support students.
- Provide laptops, Kindles or iPads for work completion.

Chapter Eight

Integrating Inclusive Trends into Schools

The case studies herein discuss administrators' inclusion perceptions and practices from the elementary to the high school environment as well as district office and a state Department of Education. With educational experience ranging from fourteen to forty-one years, participants work in different size schools including small schools whereby the district is comprised of a few hundred students to large schools responsible for thousands of students. Each region has its unique populations, challenges and approaches.

Many interviewees experienced arriving at a school where the situation was dire. Disgruntled employees were exhausted from working with students who did not seem to care and parents who were unsupportive. Many staff members felt beat down and ready to give up. Test scores had tanked, resources were scant, technology was lacking and spirits were low. Some schools were under improvement and others were in danger of being taken over.

Other administrators fare better as they work with a more privileged population. The budget is not as tight or, if it is, parents are able to contribute funds that pick up the fiscal slack. Certain regions are small enough that a sense of community remains strong; thus surrounding businesses regularly contribute resources and donate tangible goods when called upon to do so. Some administrators have a stronger tax base than others. Desiring success for every student, all administrators, regardless of their challenges, have to determine the most effective way to include their exceptional student population while ensuring teachers are properly trained, resources are adequate and the curriculum is rigorous.

Small schools face a unique set of challenges. Due to budget cuts, many small schools have had to transition to a four-day school week. The inability to acquire ancillary staff in rural areas where large budgets are nonexistent has sometimes resulted in searching for online Skype-type solutions. Similarly, online courses are established to provide students with opportunities to take courses to which they might otherwise not be privy. Often only able to attain teachers who possess alternative certification, administrators must hire teachers who are frequently ill-equipped to handle their many classroom responsibilities. These alternatively certificated teachers generally require a plethora of additional training and outright "babysitting."

Regardless of the school level, school ranking or student population, all administrators must decide how their staff is going to meet the needs of their students. Far more than a faceless number on a data sheet, there is a keen awareness that educators mold students and prepare them to become productive members of society. Structuring a framework that results in buy-in from teachers is a challenge for everyone. Developing and sharing a clear vision that ensures all staff members know the expectations requires thoughtful assessment of where each respective school or district is and where they hope to head. Only then can a clear path be created for everyone to collectively travel.

Some administrators educate their general education staff on special education issues by administering a special education acronym and procedure pretest to staff. The results reveal how much they do or do not know about special education terms and processes. This pretest exercise is followed by distributing a copy of terms and definitions to which staff can refer during the year. Thus, the pretest alerts staff to the deficiencies they have regarding special education processes and the handout provides information to help remediate those gaps.

Several administrators are now scheduling time for various therapists to speak with faculty about the services they provide and how their interventions are relevant to what students need while in the classroom environment. Similarly, psychologists or special education department chairs discuss how a student's label is manifested in various content or social contexts. Most administrators ensure their teachers have a copy of their students' IEPs (or at a minimum the accommodations page) and that case workers or the students' teacher from the prior year explain the nuances of the child's disability. This includes a discussion about what does and does not work for an individual student. The accommodations page is placed in the teachers' plan book and the substitute teacher's file. Staff members are made aware that failure to follow an IEP puts the teacher and district personnel at risk for a lawsuit.

Most administrators believe their school or district appropriately identifies exceptional students. This ameliorates misidentifying economically disadvantaged populations or those whose first language is not English. Economically disadvantaged students are assisted via the current response to intervention strategies while English language learners' issues are identified and their needs are addressed via the language assessment.

To properly implement inclusion, some administrators research the practices of successful schools and emulate them. Identifying and hiring quality teachers while utilizing staff members' talents and skills occurs systematically. Various experts who possess invaluable knowledge regarding the inclusion and co-teaching models are sought. A conscious effort to stay current on inclusive practices occurs. An emphasis on all students being treated as "ours" instead of "yours" and "mine" is made. Administrative self-assessments determine if faculty members are being led and issues are being addressed in the manner hoped.

When able, administrators partner master teachers into co-teaching teams and support inclusion through systematic, scheduled collaboration and in-services. Newer teachers have opportunities to observe master teachers in classroom settings with the goal of modeling effective instruction. Providing teachers with opportunities to try new strategies within acceptable parameters encourages ownership. A means for teachers to affect occupational and job shadowing opportunities is provided.

Learning across the curriculum occurs by developing co-teaching academies through which content teachers collaboratively develop lesson plans that support each other. For instance, the mathematics teacher might be teaching time and distance, so the social studies teacher discusses how far it is from one town to the next and asks how fast a person might get there walking three miles per hour or how fast someone on horseback might get there riding twenty miles per hour. The English teacher supports the social studies teacher by assisting with research.

Programming occurs with the focus on student growth. Most administrators ensure struggling students are provided with opportunities to participate in courses in which they can experience success by placing them with teachers who have the skills and talents to educate them. Most administrators implement the partial-inclusion model; however, very few schools are implementing a true co-teaching model in which one full-time general and one full-time special educator work together on a daily basis due to budgetary constraints.

For those schools where co-teaching does exist, teams are often partnered via a volunteer process. Volunteers are usually paired based on compatibility and the skills each partner possesses. The goal is for each team member to enhance their colleague's classroom instruction. Co-teaching teams collaboratively determine how classroom responsibilities will be divided. Administrators usually schedule the student population as 1:3 special to general education students. To prevent burnout, teams have the option to rotate at the end of every year.

On many campuses, special educators still teach some special education content classes. Examples include consumer math so students can balance a checkbook or resource English so students can learn basic vocabulary words. However, exceptional student support for core content areas also occurs during resource time. That is, students bring work from their general education classrooms and obtain additional time and explanation to complete it during resource time.

Most administrators agree there is no need to have a dedicated counselor for the exceptional student population. Although doing so may enable the counselor to better know the student, this arrangement is viewed as segregating the school into "yours" and "mine." This in turn leads to the perception that "those" students aren't a part of the "regular" student body. Thus, spreading the counseling responsibility among all counselors models the fact that all students belong to the school.

Systemic improvement occurs when professional development days are utilized effectively and the budget supports quality instruction. Administrators visit classrooms, identify patterns and ascertain the support that may be needed. Library shelves are stocked with information at all levels including advanced reading material to meet the needs of the often neglected gifted and high-performing students. Furthermore, classrooms are leveled, enabling teachers to work with students who are at the same stage of learning.

Professional development has many faces. At times, outside experts are hired to in-service staff; other times district or school personnel provide the training. In some instances ancillary staff, instructional aides, counselors and teachers are included in certified staff trainings to ensure everyone is aware of updated strategies. Refresher training occurs periodically; there are no assumptions that teachers remember what they were taught in a prior workshop. New teachers have a mentor in their grade or subject area their first year in the district. Everyone understands that accommodations are legal requirements, not options.

The most challenging students are usually placed in a self-contained environment with certified, highly qualified teachers until they can demonstrate the ability to comply with school rules. They are then slowly transitioned into general education classrooms. Strategies to support emotional behavioral disordered students and those students on the autism spectrum scale are preplanned. As these students transition into general education classrooms, care is given to divide them among the various co-teaching classrooms avoiding their placement with teachers who are new to education. Positive behavioral supports are incorporated into student programming as needed. To help all students manage behaviors, some administrators are adopting a leadership program such as "The 7 Habits of Highly Effective Teens" or the restorative practices educational approach. Everybody is trained including administrators, students and staff.

Ideally, administrators map and repeatedly discuss their vision of what inclusion should look like. They discuss pertinent issues with team members to ensure everyone is on board. They encourage their teachers to generate new and fresh ideas. When inclusion is initially discussed, they provide time for teachers to digest the need and implication of implementing inclusive strategies. Concerns such as how nonverbal cognitively impaired students should be graded is often alleviated when teachers learn they can administer pass/fail grades as appropriate.

Effective inclusion programs are built from the bottom-up rather than the top-down (although support must come from the top). This avoids teachers feeling imposed upon, lays the groundwork before implementation and con-tributes to the feeling of ownership. Some administrators bring in teachers from other schools who have implemented inclusion to describe the process and what does or does not work.

Most administrators provide staff support via an open-door policy. Many meet with all staff members weekly or bi-monthly and collaborate with indi-vidual or small groups as needed. While in faculty meetings, teachers are encouraged to share their successes so everyone can learn and grow. Some administrators opt to meet with teachers, paraprofessionals and therapists separately so they can discuss issues specific to them. Furthermore, campus administrators meet regularly to address programmatic operational concerns or issues. A vast number of mechanisms are in place to address issues as they occur.

One of the biggest changes occurring with ancillary services is the partici-pation of therapists in classrooms. Occupational, physical, and speech lan-guage therapists are not just consulting or working with students on a pull-out basis; they are observing and working with students in the classroom environment. This gives therapists a better sense of how the child negotiates their physical environment or how responses and interactions ensue when with peers. Suggestions are then made to the teacher regarding how the disability impacts the student and by what means the teacher can specifically support the student to assist the child or remediate gaps.

Instructional aides (IAs) no longer reside only in resource rooms. They are often floating from classroom to classroom supporting students who need them most. They also participate in study hall instruction and supervision and help tutor students before and after school. Administrators need to ensure that teachers know how to best utilize IAs within their environment. For instance, in some cases IAs need to accompany an upset student to a prede-termined area or person so the student can deescalate. Other times IAs can work with small groups of students or sit near a behaviorally at-risk student.

Data, not derived from standardized tests alone, provides trends and is used as a baseline from which improvement can be determined. Academic data that divides information into useable subgroups is often gathered and distributed in the fall, winter and spring. This data is utilized to correctly place incoming students and to consistently guide decisions by implementing stop-gap measures. All staff members need to be trained to use data in a way that helps them optimally assist students. Furthermore, administrators need to share data that shows academic gains and discipline reductions so staff members are aware of the payoff for their efforts.

Some administrators coach their teachers on multiple ways that their peers can be used to support their classmates. The goal is to assign peer tutors to their tutee according to the tutors' strengths and the tutees' needs. In some instances, general education tutors place the homework of a disorganized exceptional student in the homework basket. Other tutors are paired with special education peers to review for tests, read, play games and socialize. Teachers must ensure tutors do not miss valuable class instruction because they are tutoring a struggling classmate.

Prior to the school year beginning, some administrators schedule every parent for a fifteen-minute parent-teacher conference to review classroom expectations and school policies. As the year progresses, many administrators ensure parents are kept in the loop via a weekly school newsletter or by establishing a specific day of the week the parent can expect a folder from the school, for example "Wednesday's Folders." Where budgets allow, a phone-calling system that automatically sends messages or announcements can be procured.

Most administrators acknowledge the need to consider the diverse population that all teachers work with when conducting teacher evaluations; this is especially true of included classrooms. The level and effectiveness of instruction as it relates to the students in the classroom is measured, as well as the consistency of checking for understanding and student engagement. Administrators often provide feedback during or after classroom visits in both verbal and written form recognizing that verbal conversation incentivizes and motivates while written documentation provides evidence of teacher engagement, congruency and response. Many incorporate reflection and conclude with the all-important pat on the back.

To conclude, administrators believe that inclusion has a positive impact on exceptional students who realize that they are just as capable of performing academically as their peers; they don't need to be coddled. They are now "students," not "the exceptional students" or "from the exceptional class" or "the exceptional group." People see them as being part of the school, not as a separate entity. Furthermore, data shows test scores, grades and attendance improve while inappropriate behavior and suspensions decrease.

Similarly, administrators assert that inclusion has a positive impact on general education students for they become more accepting and tolerant of others with differences. General education students grow to understand that everyone is unique and possess different abilities, strengths and weaknesses.

Moreover, general education students who may be academically at risk benefit from the inclusion co-teaching model because they now have two teachers who present coursework material using different methods. Students might also be exposed to alternative procedures when analyzing problems because they are receiving instruction from two teachers with different backgrounds and presentation styles.

Administrators also state that inclusion has a positive impact on general education teachers when they collaborate and orchestrate a well-developed lesson. General educators are exposed to and learn certain aspects about exceptional students that they didn't previously know before being involved in the co-teaching model. Skill-sets and responsibilities are shared, and working with diverse students helps educators hone their craft. On the one hand, exceptional students make some general educators feel intruded upon as working with this population is unfamiliar territory. Being the teacher of record causes stress as it disrupts the established flow of the classroom. Yet, after working in an inclusive environment for about a year, general educators tend to see the value in the inclusion program as they see the growth of the student and the impact they had as a teacher.

Finally, administrators reason that inclusion has a positive impact on special education teachers. Special educators are interacting more frequently with general education colleagues, entering their classrooms to consult, collaborate and provide assistance as needed. Special educators feel like they are a valuable part of the school because they are able to maximize their talents. However, the inclusion model has created more work for special educators who must reach out to several general education colleagues and provide supports in multiple classrooms. Being asked to work with and be responsible for all students in addition to IEP responsibilities, while being required to learn the general education curriculum, can be daunting. Nevertheless, not being the sole person responsible for the students' education is a positive.

Including exceptional students into classrooms with their general education peers is a model that can be immensely successful when consistently supported by administrators who have vision and direction. Although the initial transition to inclusion may seem like a formidable task, when done thoughtfully and methodically, the practice is sound. Learn from your colleagues, then adapt or creatively develop strategies that will catapult your faculty and students to success.

Index

About the Author

Dr. Faith Andreasen has over twenty years of educational experience teaching elementary through college level students. She served as department chair for special education and has mentored graduate students in leadership and special education courses. Formerly an associate professor of research at Northcentral University, Dr. Andreasen is currently an adjunct professor for Morningside College. She has been published in several peer-reviewed journals and is an alternative dispute resolution mediator.

www.ingramcontent.com/pod-product-compliance
Lightning Source LLC
Chambersburg PA
CBHW050522280326
41932CB00014B/2419